EXISTENTIALISM
FOR BEGINNERS

EXISTENTIALISM
FOR BEGINNERS

BY **DAVID COGSWELL**
ILLUSTRATIONS BY **JOE LEE**

FOR BEGINNERS®

an imprint of Steerforth Press
Hanover, New Hampshire

For Beginners LLC
62 East Starrs Plain Road
Danbury, CT 06810 USA
www.forbeginnersbooks.com

A For Beginners® Documentary Comic Book
Copyright © 2008

Cataloging-in-Publication information is available from the Library of Congress.

ISBN # 978-1-934389-21-8 Trade

Manufactured in the United States of America

For Beginners® and Beginners Documentary Comic Books® are published
by For Beginners LLC.

First Edition

10 9 8 7 6 5 4 3 2 1

Table of Contents

People say that what we're all seeking is the meaning of life . . . I think that what we're really seeking is the experience of being alive.

—Rudyard Kipling

Existentialism:
What's in a Name?

No one ever owned existentialism. It has always meant different things to different people. It was never a single doctrine that was laid down definitively by one person or group. Each piece of writing about it is different, each bears an individual stamp. There was no single voice of authority, so its definition has always had blurry edges. It grew up in the public domain, as a dawning of a new way of thinking about life that emerged at a particular moment in history. It could be seen as a historical necessity or inevitability, an effort to adapt to a new confluence of cultural and historical forces.

The list of so-called existentialists is very diverse, ranging from devout Catholics, Protestants, and Jews to agnostics and staunch atheists, and includes a variety of nationalities, temperaments and personal beliefs. Most of those referred to today as existentialists were not even alive when the word was created. And most of those who were alive objected to being categorized that way.

They tended to be mavericks, outsiders of the philosophical academy who wrote in untraditional forms, like fiction, plays or essays as well as more traditional philosophical treatises. Yet as diverse as they are, there are certain affinities among them that justify grouping them together as purveyors of an existentialist view. Their greatest similarity may be their own strong devotion to individualism, and their emphasis of the individual in discussing philosophical subjects.

It may be easier to understand existentialism by thinking of it not as a coherent system of philosophy, but as a widespread rebellion against traditional philosophy, which many felt was out of touch with real life. Existential philosophy left a rich vein of literature, colored by a new world view, representing a new historical phase in the intellectual and moral evolution of Western civilization.

Defining Terms

Webster's Collegiate Dictionary defines existentialism as "a chiefly 20th century philosophy that is centered upon the analysis of existence specifically of individual human beings, that regards human existence as not exhaustively describable or understandable in idealistic or scientific terms, and that stresses the freedom and responsibility of the individual, the irreducible uniqueness of an ethical or religious situation, and usually the isolation and subjective experiences (as of anxiety, guilt, dread, anguish) of an individual therein."

Webster defines the root word existential as "1. of, relating to, or affirming existence. 2. a. grounded in existence or the experience of existence, having being in time and space." And its third meaning is its specific use as it evolved in relation to the context of existential philosophy: "concerned with or involving an individual as radically free and responsible."

The Dawning of a New Awareness

The emergence of existential philosophy in the nineteenth and twentieth centuries could be seen as an attempt to stretch traditional ways of thinking to accommodate emerging discoveries that were irreversibly expanding man's view of the universe.

The discoveries and advances of science, technology and exploration were drastically expanding and changing the way people perceived and understood the world. The discovery of dinosaurs, as just one example, introduced realities that could not be accommodated by the traditional religious view of the universe and its origin. Dinosaurs were not in the Book of Genesis. The Biblical view of the world created in six days was shattered when people were suddenly struck with the fact that the earth had a long history and had evolved over inconceivable stretches

of time. A flood of similarly earthshattering new realities presented themselves to Western Civilization forcing prevailing systems of thinking to stretch to accommodate them.

A greater understanding of time and duration brought attention to the failure of traditional logic and rationality to accommodate the passage of time. The logic that had prevailed in the western world, that of Plato and Descartes, was exercised as if from a point of view outside of place and time. Objectivity, which requires mentally placing oneself outside of that which is being discussed, was seen as the most valid and reliable way of thinking. Existential philosophy grew from the feeling that a new, more agile kind of reasoning was needed, one that could accommodate the movement of time, the expanding universe and the increasing power in the hands of mankind.

With the increase in scientific knowledge came an increased power over the material world. Though scientific knowledge could create the power, it could not create solutions for all of the problems brought on by the exercise of that power. Human systems, which had become increasingly powerful and efficient were powerless to avert the catastrophic destruction and carnage of the World Wars, for example. Science was a method, a very powerful one, for processing information and gathering reliable knowledge. But while science increasingly supplanted religion as the dominant belief system, science had no ethical component.

In a world where many had ceased to believe in God, humanity needed new ways to decide what is ethical, what is permissible. Science, with its cold objectivity, lacked the human dimension, so it failed as an all-encompassing belief system that could guide human judgment and action.

From the ruins of religion

Existentialism grew up within the void left by the decline of religion. It's difficult in the twenty-first century to grasp how much religion ruled the lives of people in Medieval Europe. As William Barrett explains in his book *Rational Man: A Study in Existential Philosophy*, religion was for Medieval man "not so much a theological system as a solid psychological matrix surrounding the individual's life from birth to death, sanctifying and enclosing all its ordinary and extraordinary occasions in sacrament and ritual. The loss of the Church was the loss of a whole system of symbols, images, dogmas and rites which had the psychological validity of immediate experience, and within which hitherto the whole psychic life of Western man had been safely contained. In losing religion, man lost the concrete connection with a transcendental realm of being; he was set free to deal with this world in all its brute objectivity."

The Renaissance and the Enlightenment uprooted traditional religious beliefs, and replaced them with science, rationalism and materialism. Logical positivism, a philosophy based on science as the ultimate way of knowing, became elevated as religion shrank in influence. The scientific view was built on several principles.

- Rationalism—the belief that logic and intellectual processes are the only reliable ways of knowing or judging, emphasis on the objective over the subjective.

- Materialism—the idea that all that exists is matter, material, substance, there is no such thing as spirit, and thinking is just an electro-chemical activity in the brain.

- Empiricism—the emphasis on sensory, tangible, measurable experience as a way of knowing and validating knowledge.

- Reductionism—the explanation of things by breaking them into their simplest parts, as an improvement over the Medieval practice of explaining phenomena in terms of spiritual forces.

Descartes, the French philosopher largely responsible for establishing the scientific method, recognized its limited applicability. A profoundly religious man, Descartes advocated separating areas in which the scientific method is appropriate from areas of human activity in which it is not adequate. As science became enthroned as the new religion, many subjective or metaphysical concerns that fell outside of its realm by definition, were simply cast aside as unreal or irrelevant.

Though science was bringing a flood of knowledge and power to humanity, existential thinkers said that science and strictly rational thinking did not address the whole of life, only the measurable part. Many human needs and concerns, such as morals and ethics, love and devotion, and mortality were not addressed by science. If such a thing as love were to be recognized by science, it would only be to measure or analyze it from the point of view of an outside observer. Unlike religion, which had infused each part of life with ritual and meaning, science proved inadequate as an overarching system of existence for human beings. It left many issues unaddressed. And that which fell outside the reach of science, that which could not be scientifically proven, was considered to not exist.

The tendency to separate the intellect and place it above the rest of life had a long history, going back to the beginning of Western philosophy when Plato set the intellect apart from the rest of life and made it the ruler. While philosophers in the academies pondered and debated increasingly abstract questions such as whether the world exists, or whether the person thinking exists, they became less relevant to people outside of the academy.

In the early nineteenth century, Hegel's idealism took the tendency to separate the intellect from the rest of life to its extreme. He created an elaborate system that supposedly explained everything in terms of the evolution of what he called Mind or Spirit and painted a picture of a universe in which he found a rational, secular replacement for religion at the center of human life.

Viewing the world from such an abstract point of view could lead to catastrophes, in which individual people fall through the cracks of a grand theory. The reaction to this idealistic trend of academic philosophy became known as existential philosophy, and in the 1940s that tradition was elevated to an "ism": existentialism.

Philosophy matters

Existential philosophers wanted to pull philosophy down from the ivory towers of the academy and bring it to the real life of people in the streets. Defined as the inquiry into ways of thinking and understanding the world, philosophy does make a difference in how people actually live. Philosophy tries to understand the basic logic that underlies the way people think.

For example, some who believe in the Darwinian theory of natural selection, what Samuel Butler called "survival of the fittest," believe that it is wrong to help those in need because helping the weak survive will weaken the species in the evolutionary process. "Social Darwinism" referred to a political belief system that justified policies of individual self interest based on Darwin's theory of natural selection.

On the other hand, if one believes the unit of survival in the evolutionary process is the community, one may believe that society is best served by policies through which members of the community work together and help each other. If one has studied ecology, one may believe their own survival is dependant on the survival of many other species of plants and animals, so that care of the environment is a part of their own strategy for survival. The way people think does affect the way people will live and conduct their affairs in a given society.

If one believes that sin will lead to burning in Hell for eternity, he or she may think differently about morals and ethics than one who believes there is no such thing as Hell, or even God. Philosophy does make a material difference in people's lives. Even ideas we are not conscious of may underlie our behavior and affect the way society works.

Existentialists believed that western philosophy, the way people thought, had gotten off track, civilization had lost its way and was leading humanity toward dangerous confrontations with new realities. The massive human catastrophes of the World Wars seemed to dampen the great confidence of the Western world in its science and its powers and to affirm the fear that man had unleashed forces beyond his control.

Existential philosophers challenged some of the fundamental beliefs that had prevailed in western civilization and looked for new ways of thinking that would better accommodate what happens in real life.

In the Beginning Was (Not) the Word

The origin of the word existentialism is itself controversial. It surfaced in the popular culture of France in the euphoric first days of liberation after World War II and four grim years of occupation under the iron heel of the Nazis. The angular, exotic word, associated with the daring, colorful and sexy café culture of postwar France, captured the imagination of the world and spread rapidly, even though few had a clear idea what it meant.

Though the word is often attributed to Jean Paul Sartre, he clearly did not coin the term. When a reporter

9

asked him in August 1945 if he was an existentialist he said, "I don't know what that means. Mine is a philosophy of being." But two months later, in October of that year, he changed his tune and embraced the word in a lecture called "Existentialism is a Humanism," in which he laid out the philosophy he had just begun to call existentialism. Sartre became the person most identified with existentialism.

Some say Gabriel Marcel coined the word in 1940 to refer to the work of Sartre and Simone de Beauvoir. In 1960 Beauvoir said, "During a discussion organized during the summer [of 1945] ... Sartre had refused to allow Gabriel Marcel to apply this adjective to him ... I shared his irritation. I had written my novel [The Blood of Others] before I had even encountered the term existentialism; my inspiration came from my own experience, not from a system. But our protests were in vain. In the end, we took the epithet that everyone used for us and used it for our own purposes."

According to Karl Jaspers, in his three-volume Philosophy, "[I] thought I was inventing a word, 'existentialism,' to describe a possible decay of self-elucidation. After the war I was surprised to see this realized in France. I did not pursue or anticipate the road of this later existentialism."

Some say it was the French writer Louis Lavelle who coined the term. Some have said the word emerged from the public domain, and it's quite likely more than one person hit upon the idea of adding of an "ism" to the word "existential," to refer to the "existential philosophy" that was based on Soren Kierkegaard's use the word.

In any case, once existentialism had been named and associated with a group of writers identified with the French underground resistance, including Sartre, Albert Camus, de Beauvoir, Maurice Merleau Ponty and Marcel himself, the word was then applied retroactively to the predecessors of those writers. The tradition was extended backward in time to include Martin Heidegger and Karl Jaspers earlier in the twentieth century, and back to the early nineteenth century to Friedrich Nietzsche and Soren Kierkegaard.

Also identified as existentialists were German poet Rainer Maria Rilke, Austrian fiction writer Franz Kafka, Spanish writer and political activist José Ortega y Gasset, as well as Maurice Merleau-Ponty, Martin Buber, Paul Tillich, Eugene Gendlin, playwrights Harold Pinter and Samuel Beckett and many more. The American Beat Generation writers, such as Jack Kerouac and Allen Ginsberg, have also been identified with the existentialists.

The label was applied to more and more writers and artists until Sartre himself, the man most identified with existentialism, eventually said it had been so broadly applied that "it no longer means anything anymore."

According to Tillich, the broad extension of the word was appropriate because the ideas underlying existentialism became increasingly relevant as the world evolved. "In contrast to the situation in the last three years after the second World War," he wrote, "when most people identified existentialism with Sartre, it is now common knowledge in this country that existentialism in the western intellectual history starts with Pascal in the seventeenth century, has an underground history in the eighteenth century, a revolutionary history in the nineteenth century and an astonishing victory in the twentieth century. Existentialism has become the style of our period in all realms of life."

The Origins of Existentialism

Most scholars trace existential philosophy back to Soren Kierkegaard, a troubled Danish writer in the early nineteenth century. Kierkegaard rebelled against the prevailing church of his time, which he found to have lost the spirit of Christianity and become just a secular institution with no soul, and also against the grand system idealistic philosophy of Georg Wilhelm Friedrich Hegel, considered at that time by the academic establishment to be the epitome of philosophical thinking. Kierkegaard ridiculed Hegel's system, proclaiming that "an existential system is impossible" and declaring that no system of thought could ever adequately explain or predict life.

The other most-cited originator of existentialism was a German contemporary of Kierkegaard, a philologist-turned-philosopher named Friedrich Nietzsche. Though he developed his thinking independently of Kierkegaard, Nietzche's thinking was remarkably similar in spirit to that of Kierkegaard even though Nietzsche was as passionate an atheist as Kierkegaard was a Christian. Both thought prevailing religious and philosophical institutions were inadequate to the spiritual needs of the new world.

Karl Jaspers, one of the main articulators of existential philosophy in the twentieth century, wrote in his book *Man in the Modern Age*, that the rise of existential philosophy represents the struggle by modern man to lead an authentic and genuine life in spite of the modern drift toward mass, standardized society. Jaspers sees the flowering of existentialism as coming forth from Kierkegaard and Nietzsche independently.

Jaspers could be credited with bringing together the work of Kierkegaard and Nietzsche for the twentieth century and outlining the unified ground of the existential philosophers in his book *Existenzphilosophie*. But he objected to the label "existentialism" when it arose later in France because it seemed to denote a school of thought, a doctrine, which he saw as a limitation.

JASPERS: *Kierkegaard and Nietzsche appear as the expression of destinies, destinies which nobody noticed then, with the exception of some ephemeral and immediately forgotten presentiments, but which they themselves already comprehended...*

This comparison is all the more important since there could have been no influence of one upon the other, and because their very differences make their common features so much more impressive. Their affinity is so compelling, from the whole course of their lives down to the individual details of their thought, that their nature seems to have been elicited by the necessities of the spiritual situation of their times. With them a shock occurred to Western philosophizing whose final meaning can not yet be estimated.

Common to both of them is a type of thought and humanity which was indissolubly connected with a moment of this epoch, and so understood by them... Their thinking created a good atmosphere. They passed beyond all of the limits then regarded as obvious. It is as if they no longer shrank back from anything in thought. Everything permanent was as if consumed in a dizzying suction...

In a magnificent way, penetrating a whole life with the earnestness of philosophizing, they brought forth not some doctrines, not any basic position, not some picture of the world, but rather a new total intellectual attitude for men...

The fact that one was a passionate Christian and the other a passionate atheist was not as important to Jaspers as the fact that they both rooted their thinking not in the abstract realms of the academy, but in their *existenz*.

Walter Kauffman, in his 1956 book *Existentialism from Dostoyevsky to Sartre*, chose as his starting point the Russian novelist Fyodor Dostoyevsky, a Greek Orthodox Christian whose novels produced some of the most eloquent statements of existential philosophy.

Sartre himself traced the origin of existentialism to Dostoyevsky's statement, "If God didn't exist, everything would be permissible." Some scholars have said the first piece of existentialist literature was the poem "Pensees," written by Blaise Pascal, who lived 1623-1662. In his 1959 book *From Shakespeare to Existentialism*, Kauffman identified precursors of existentialism going back to Shakespeare in the 1500s.

Nietzsche, Heidegger and Martin Buber, all major contributors to existential thinking, turned all the way back to ancient Greek philosophers such as Heraclitus to rediscover what they felt had been lost in Greek philosophy with Plato.

And yet, as much diversity as the existential tradition reflects, existentialism represents a common thread in history, a broad-based rebellion against traditional philosophy, especially the idealist and rationalist philosophy epitomized by Georg Wilhelm Friedrich Hegel and the increasing abstraction of philosophy that had over the centuries taken it farther and farther from the concerns of real people.

What Unites Them

As diverse as the existentialist writers were, there are a number of basic principles they share in common.

COMMANDMENTS NOT EXACTLY, BUT RULES MAYBE.

- Existentialism focuses attention and concern on the individual over the group, mass type or category, on the specific over the general, actual events and experience over the ideas, theories, statistics or imaginary events. To achieve an authentic life, an individual must direct oneself and resist the pressure of mass society to create standardized human beings.

- Rationality is imperfect and unreliable without the guidance and tempering of other more intuitive faculties. Real human life will always go beyond the boundaries of any rational system we can construct to explain it, predict it or control it. Though rational thought is an extremely valuable tool, it does not provide answers to all of life's problems.

- There is no fixed definition of a human being. We define ourselves through our choices and actions. We find ourselves in the world, existing in a particular situation, but must go forward from there to create ourselves. Though we find ourselves in an absurd, indifferent world, there is some hope for redemption in that we have the power to be creators of our own lives, and are responsible for what we do and what we are.

- Human beings cannot meaningfully contemplate the universe from any point of reference other than that of a mortal human being. Rational thinking has the tendency to take place in an imaginary world in which the thinker assumes the position of an omniscient, immortal being, which is of limited value because we are in actuality mortal and suffer the problems of all mortal beings, and die. Unfortunately real life eventually breaks into our thoughts.

In *Existentialism For Beginners*, we'll pour over the rich literature, history and ideas behind existentialism, how it was born in the nineteenth century, grew up in the early twentieth century and became all the rage in the post World War II years, how it infused the culture at large and why it is still significant in the twenty-first century.

Georg Wilhelm Friedrich Hegel

(August 27, 1770–November 4, 1831)
Since existentialism was a rebellion against idealist philosophy, Georg Wilhelm Friedrich Hegel, the pinnacle of idealism, is a good place to start. Hegel was the status quo existentialism rebelled against.

Hegel was born to a middle class family in Stuttgart, Germany, the son of a civil servant. He was encouraged in his intellectual pursuits by his unusually progressive mother and educated in a Protestant seminary. He became a professor and very popular university lecturer. His lectures on aesthetics, the philosophy of science, religion and history were published and he published a number of books, including *The Science of Logic*, *The Encyclopedia of the Philosophical Sciences*, and the most important one, in which he lays out what he called absolute idealism: *The Phenomenology of Mind* (also translated as *The Phenomenology of Spirit* because English translators disagree on whether the German word *geist* means "mind" or "spirit". Hegel defined "spirit" closely to "reason" or "mind").

Hegel's philosophy brought to its apex a trend that went back to the point at which Plato separated the intellect from the rest of the human being and placed it at the top of the hierarchy of values. The widespread popularity of Hegel's philosophy represented the final victory of the intellect, rationality and science over all.

The World System

Hegel's idealism envisioned the world as a grand march toward the fulfillment of a superhuman collective reality. It was a grand sweeping view of history leading toward a great climax. All the loose ends, all the details were swept under the rug to create an image of the grand procession of life in which the world was progressing toward a state of perfect union with "the world spirit."

The world spirit sounds a lot like God and it seems a little like religion with one set of gods replaced with another, and that would not be too out of character because as a young man Hegel was somewhat of a mystic. He believed that the mind constructed reality. His philosophical ideas were inspired by religious ideas. He was a Christian who tried to do for Protestants what Thomas Aquinas had done as a Catholic, to reconcile religion with reason, to create a logical system that justifies or explains religion.

Hegel wanted to interpret the contradictions of life as part of an evolving rational system that aspired to an ultimate goal. He disagreed with Immanuel Kant's statement that there is a limit to what can be known. Hegel said all things are knowable, whatever exists can be known. In Hegel's system, everything could be known, everything was logical. It was the formal declaration of the absolute supremacy of the intellect.

I GOT THE WHOLE WORLD SYSTEM IN MY HANDS. I GOT THE ...

"Reason governs the world and has consequently governed its history," he said. Individual passions exist to be a part of the universal progression of life, "to produce the edifice of human society."

His statement that "the real is the rational and the rational is the real" was a paraphrasing of a supposition that had underpinned Western philosophy from the time of the ancient Greeks when Parmenides said, "It is the same thing that can be thought and that can be. What can't be thought, can't be real."

YEAH, I KNOW "THE REAL IS RATIONAL AND THE RATIONAL IS REAL", BUT I ALSO KNOW I CAN'T GET A DECENT CUP OF COFFEE IN 19TH CENTURY GERMANY.

He built his system through what he called the dialectic. He began with Being, the most fundamental concept, as his thesis. In the dialectic, the thesis gives birth to its opposite, in this case the concept of Nothing, the antithesis of Being. The interaction of the two was a new concept that reconciles the two: Becoming.

The dialectic of history, according to Hegel, ultimately leads to absolute spirit or mind.

His conception of history only encompassed Western civilization, which was the world he knew. He simplified history into a simple linear progression from the Greeks and the Romans through his contemporary Europe. He saw the history of the East as the background to the Greeks.

Through his dialectic and the concept of Becoming, Hegel introduced time into the concept of human existence. Man and the universe are not fixed, he suggested, they are in a state of change, of evolving toward something greater. The universe is like an organism that is realizing itself.

19

The Ultimate State

Hegel dealt with the largest questions. He started his philosophy of history by asking: What is the purpose of the world? And his answer was that the purpose of the progression of history is to realize the idea of spirit or absolute mind. All of our individual interests and volitions are merely part of bringing about that great universal order, he asserted. The individual exists to further the development of the whole, the World Spirit (*weltgeist*). World historical men, like Caesar and Napoleon, are those who "grasp just such a higher universal, make it their own purpose, and realize this purpose in accordance with the higher law of the spirit."

He saw the State, as the expression of the Ultimate Spirit. The greatest achievements of human beings, he said, are only possible through collective social structures. He did not say that all states as they exist are truly expressions of Ultimate Spirit, but that ideally the state can be that expression. And that is the only way for humankind to realize itself.

"Heroes" like Caesar, though they had their own personal agendas, were agents of the World Spirit. "World historical agents" could not be held to the same standards of morality as normal individuals. "They stand outside of morality." The highest aim of mankind is to become the state. The world is evolving to a perfect state, and when it arrives at that point, history will cease. "The state is the divine Idea as it exists on earth," he said.

The ideals were the starting point, specific instances would have to be fit into the categories, and that would apply to people. There was not much room in his system for the individual. "The individual does not invent his own content," he wrote, "he is what he is by acting out the universal as his own content."

The purpose of human beings is to realize their destiny in becoming a state, he said. "Freedom is nothing but the recognition and adoption of such universal substantial objects as Right and Law and the production of a reality which is in accordance with them – the State."

Mussolini's writings in 1932 drew heavily from Hegel: "The foundation of Fascism is the conception of the State, its character, its duty, and its aim. Fascism conceives of the State as an absolute, in comparison with which all individuals or groups are relative, only to be conceived of in their relation to the State."

Hegel asserted that finite qualities are not fully real because they depend on other finite qualities to determine them. But qualitative infinity would be more self-determining and therefore more real. Finite, natural things are less real because they are less self-determining than spiritual things.

BUT I REALLY DO LIKE HIM.

Not only did the fascists parrot Hegel. His ideas also had a profound influence on the German philosopher Karl Marx, and on the Russian revolutionaries Lenin and Stalin. According to linguist and political activist Noam Chomsky, Hegel's ideas about collective entities with greater rights than individuals were appropriated by "neo-Hegelians" and used as the ideological basis of fascism, communism, and corporations. It seems unlikely that Hegel could have envisioned such applications of his ideas, but the ideas still have a powerful influence on the world in the twenty-first century.

BUT — REALLY I AM ALL ABOUT THE FREEDOM.

Hegel himself did not believe in totalitarianism. His idea of the state was one whose powers were limited to that which enhance the freedom of its members. The ideal state was founded on a universal and rational law that safeguarded the interests of every individual, no matter their social status. He condemned "slavery and serfdom and the disqualification from owning property, or the prevention of its use or the like, and the deprivation of intelligent rationality, of morality, ethics, and religion..."

But though his world system was supposed to have resolved all the conflicts of the universe into a single grand movement, Hegel himself was full of contradiction. Though he spoke of the ideal of liberal democracy, in real life he was a firm supporter of the Prussian monarchy. And in the democracy of his world system, individual freedom was subjugated to the supposed higher purpose of the state as an agent of the movement of history.

In his attempt to be a universal philosopher and create a philosophical system that covered all of life, he covered a lot of ground, leaving many points of contention and many ideas for others to make use of. Hegel attempted to synthesize Western philosophy up to his point, and accomplished his task to such a degree that all philosophers after him had to take him into consideration.

As Roger Kimball wrote, "It should go without saying that none of these criticisms is meant to deny that the Hegelian system possesses tremendous aesthetic appeal. The panoramic drama of absolute being struggling to achieve perfect self-knowledge in history: it is an imposing tale of a thousand and one nights for the philosophically inclined. The inconvenient question is only whether the story it tells is true. Perhaps, as Kierkegaard suggested, "Hegel was a man who had built a palace but lived in the guard house."

When the Soviet Union fell, signaling the symbolic end of the Cold War, Hegel's ideas were again resurrected, and quoted in the words of Francis Fukuyama in 1989: "What we are witnessing is not just the end of the Cold War, or a passing of a particular period of postwar history, but the end of history as such: that is, the end point of mankind's ideological evolution and the universalization of Western liberal democracy as the final form of human government." The idea caught on. But somehow history eventually resumed.

Arthur Schopenhauer

(February 22, 1788–September 21, 1860)

HEGEL? OH, I THOUGHT YOU SAID BAGEL.

While Hegel's World System dazzled much of the world, there was at least one who was unimpressed from the beginning. One of Hegel's first and most vigorous critics was Arthur Schopenhauer.

Schopenhauer was a younger contemporary of Hegel, a professor at the University of Berlin whose lectures were scarcely attended while nearly everyone flocked to Hegel's lectures held next door at the same time. Overshadowed by Hegel, he was openly contemptuous of him. Schopenhauer was not impressed with Hegel's ideas or his celebrity status, and he was not restrained in his criticism.

"Hegel, installed from above by the powers that be as the certified Great Philosopher was a flat-headed, insipid, nauseating, illiterate charlatan," said Schopenhauer, "who reached the pinnacle of audacity in scribbling together and dishing up the craziest mystifying nonsense." He complained of the "the stupefying influence of Hegel's sham wisdom," and said that no one under the age of forty should read Hegel because the danger of intellectual corruption was too great.

Idol Smasher

Today, however, it is Schopenhauer, the great iconoclast, who is the most highly read German philosopher. Though he came from the idealist tradition leading from Kant, he scoffed at where his contemporaries had taken it.

Composer Richard Wagner said that Schopenhauer finally gave voice to the secret inward belief that the world is bad. Some have written off his work as only a device to create a philosophical justification for his pessimism.

While most philosophers came from fathers who were teachers or clergymen, Schopenhauer's father was a trader, a Dutch businessman with a taste for high living. Fortunately for Arthur, his father left him independently wealthy, so he didn't have to knock around to make a living. One of his criticisms of his colleagues was that they were "too poor to be honorable and straightforward." As government employees dependent on their salaries they couldn't afford to tell a controversial truth.

The only philosophers he respected were Plato and Kant, and he respected the Hindu philosophers and combined Hinduism with Western mysticism. He was the prototypical rebel against modern, marginalized, mechanized, standardized, desensitized man. His pessimism was not cynicism, but grew out of the inner experience of the emptiness of existence as portrayed in the Hindu text *The Upanishads*.

Schopenhauer's world view is summed up in his *The World as Will and Idea*, which he published in 1818 when he was thirty. He wrote a second volume when he was fifty-five, but his views never changed from the original statement completed in his late twenties. All his subsequent writings were elaborations on his basic thesis. He accepted Kant's assertion that a human being cannot know the world, does not know "a sun and an earth, but only an eye that sees a sun and a hand that feels the earth."

Following from Kant, who followed a philosophical lineage from Hume and Descartes and back to Plato, Schopenhauer divided the world into a duality, an inner and an outer world. His outer world is "idea" or "representation", the physical world of time, space, causation, and appearance. It was what Kant called the phenomenal world. The inner world, Schopenhauer said, is will, the subjective world, not subject to the limitations of space and time, reality as opposed to appearance, Kant's noumenal world.

Every individual is the embodiment of will, and the nature of will is to strive to live. Every person is an ego whose own personal interest surpasses those of all others and the result is universal conflict. The suffering from that conflict is the normal human condition. Happiness is merely the lessening of suffering, a negative quantity.

The way out of the vicious circle, Schopenhauer suggest, is denial of the will, refusal to enter the conflict. The means to do that is in the power of the conscious intellect to understand the nature of the will and thereby transcend it, not be enslaved by it. As happiness is the absence of suffering, the ultimate good is extinction. The cure for the sickness of life is annihilation.

Schopenhauer's writings are a reflection of his own personality. He was an extremely willful and stubborn person. Rather than changing his lecture period to a time when Hegel was not also lecturing, he just quit. In 1821 he got involved in a dispute at his lodgings with a forty-seven-year-old seamstress, who he said was making too much noise, and threw her down the stairs. She sued, saying he injured her so she couldn't make a living. For five years he fought the case, till the court confiscated his property and he was forced to pay her for the rest of her life.

AND I'M
FINALLY CURED.

ARTHUR
SCHOPENHAUER
2/22/1788 -
9/21/1860

Spiritual Father

Schopenhauer launched the first foray against Hegelianism and laid a groundwork for the rebellion that became identified as existentialism. Schopenhauer was the first philosopher to inspire Nietzsche, who was thirty years old and still a philologist when Schopenhauer's *The World as Will and Idea* showed him a model for a kind of salvation that did not rely on religion. Nietzsche regarded Schopenhauer as his spiritual father, his guru, the person who ushered him into his own life as a philosopher. Nietzsche's first philosophical work was called *Schopenhauer as Educator*.

"I care for a philosopher only to the extent that he is able to be an example," wrote Nietzsche. "Kant clung to the university, subjected himself to governments, remained within the appearance of religious faith, and endured colleagues and students: it is small wonder that his example produced university professors and professors' philosophy. Schopenhauer has no consideration for the scholars' caste, stands apart, strives for independence of state and society—this is his example, his model, to begin with the most external futures..."

Schopenhauer, he said, "can be the guide to lead us out of the cave of skeptical irritation or critical resignation up to the height of a tragic view..."

Most philosophers hide in the academy, Nietzsche said, where they avoid the ultimate challenge of philosophy, which is *to understand your own life*, which could have been the mission statement of existentialism.

ALAS, POOR SCHOPENHAUER, I KNEW HIM.

Fyodor Dostoyevsky

(November 11, 1821–February 9, 1881)

Russian novelist Fyodor Dostoyevsky emerged in the nineteenth century as a new voice, a visionary who perceived long before most of his contemporaries the calamities the self-satisfied Western civilization was heading toward as the naïve belief in a coming technological utopia shattered and it became apparent that the creations of science might as easily destroy civilization as further it.

"A colossal eruption," Dostoyevsky wrote in his notebook in 1875, "a colossal eruption and all is crumbling, falling, being negated, as though it had not even existed. And not only externally, as in the West, but internally, morally."

In his "Diary of a Writer" in 1873, Dostoyevsky predicted the world was entering a "transitional period" that would be marked by profound "shocks in the life of people, doubts and negations, skepticism and vacillations regarding fundamental convictions. But with us this is more possible than anywhere else, and precisely in our times."

"Everybody is in a state of suspense," he wrote to himself in September 1876. "Everybody is alarmed; some kind of nightmare hangs over everybody; everybody has bad dreams. Just who or what this *piccola bestia* is which is causing all the upheavals is impossible to determine, because some kind of general madness is moving upon us."

Europe is changing from hour to hour, Dostoyevsky wrote in his diary in November 1877. "The fact is that we are just now on the eve of the greatest and most shocking events and upheavals in Europe, and this is said without any exaggeration ... The point is, that, to my way of thinking, the present period, too, will end in old Europe with something colossal, i.e. perhaps not literally identical with the events which brought to an end the eighteenth century, nevertheless equally gigantic, elemental and dreadful – and also entailing a change in the face of the whole world, or, at least, in the West, of Old Europe."

Anything But Rational

In his writing, Dostoyevsky crystallized the spirit and tangled with the classic problems of existentialism. *Notes from Underground* lays out the existentialist point of view, beginning with the unreliability of reason. "All these fine systems, all these theories for explaining to mankind their real normal interests..." he wrote, "are in my opinion, so far nothing but mere logical exercises." Man has, however, "such a predilection for systems and abstract deductions that he is ready to distort the truth intentionally, he is ready to deny the evidence of his senses only to justify his logic..."

Though man is enamored with logic, Dostoyevsky's narrator maintains, he is not really a logical creature. "Man has always and everywhere—whoever he may be—preferred to do as he chose, and not in the least as his reason or advantage dictated... One's own free, unfettered choice, one's own caprice, however wild it may be... is that very 'most advantageous advantage' which we have overlooked, which comes under no classification and against which all systems and theories are continually being shattered to atoms. And how do these wiseacres know that man wants a normal, a virtuous choice? What has made them conceive that man must want a rationally advantageous choice? What man wants is simply independent choice, whatever that independence may cost and wherever it may lead..."

NON LOGIC – NON SENSE – NOT FUNNY.

NO ONE WHOOPEE

30

Reason, he wrote, "is an excellent thing," but it only satisfies "the rational side of man's nature, while will is a manifestation of the whole of life, of the whole human life including reason and all the impulses. And although our life, in this manifestation of it, is often worthless, yet it is life and not simply extracting square roots. Here I, for instance, quite naturally want to live, in order to satisfy all my capacities for life, and not simply my capacity for reasoning, that is, not simply one twentieth of my capacity for life."

Contrary to Hegel's vision of history as a great plan, Dostoyevsky's Underground Man scoffed, "In short, one may say anything about the history of the world—anything that might enter the most disordered imagination. The only thing one can't say is that it's rational."

To Hell and Back

I FEEL FREE...

Dostoyevsky's own life exceeds even his own fiction. He himself went through enough harsh experiences to shatter any untested idealism. He was an epileptic who suffered grand mal seizures and lived under great financial stress practically his whole life.

He was born in Moscow only nine years after Napoleon had been driven from Russian soil. Russia was triumphant and full of promise as it looked toward the West and a new progressive era. But the country was still under the hold of a feudalistic social system with a peasant class ruled by a brutal nobility. The ideas of individual freedom that were taking hold in England and France were only beginning to be heard of in Russia. As the industrial revolution sped forward, Russian society absorbed it reluctantly as it sent a wave of social upheaval through the society.

Fyodor was one of seven children of a military doctor. The family lived in two rooms in a hospital. His mother died when he was sixteen and the father moved to the country where he owned two villages. Fyodor was sent to the Military Engineering Academy in St. Petersburg, the city founded by Peter the Great in 1703 to be his "window on Europe" as he tried to modernize Russia and integrate it with the West. The father surrounded himself with a harem, stayed drunk most of the time and tyrannized his serfs, of which he lorded over about 150, thirty of whom were male workers. His cruelty to his serfs eventually led to his murder when Fyodor was eighteen years old and attending school in St. Petersburg. The experience left a deep mark on him. Forty years later he drew upon the incident when he wrote his final work, *The Brothers Karamozov*.

Two years later, Dostoyevsky became a second lieutenant in the engineers. He remained in the army for four years, becoming increasingly wreckless and extravagant, and always in debt. He left the army in 1846 and wrote his first novel *Poor Folk*, which was an immediate critical and popular success.

He followed it with a group of short stories and two short novels, *The Double* and *The Landlady*. He began writing *Nyetochka Nyezvanova* but in 1849 the work was interrupted when he was arrested for his participation in the Petrashevsky Group, a group of intellectuals who met regularly to discuss political and social issues, adopting the ideas of liberation that were gaining currency in England and France. The group advocated a liberal reform of the social order including socialism, liberation of the serfs, and political freedom. In the reactionary climate of the time, such groups were illegal, considered conspiracy against the government. Czar Nicholas I demanded harsh punishment as an example. The members of the group were tried and sentenced to death by firing squad.

As Dostoyevsky stood with the other prisoners watching some of his associates being tied to the stake for execution, word came from an imperial messenger that his sentence had been commuted at the discretion of the Czar to exile in a prison in Siberia for four years hard labor. There Dostoyevsky wore ten-pound shackles and labored in mines and later a brick factory with murderers, thieves and other criminals. On top of the disease, brutal labor and humiliation, he was hated by the other inmates because he was seen as a member of the noble class. While there, he underwent a spiritual transformation. The only book he was allowed in prison was the New Testament, which he studied intensely. He renounced his liberal beliefs and took on the conviction that redemption comes only through suffering and faith.

After serving his four-year sentence he was freed from prison but forced to stay in Siberia and serve in the army for five years. While there he married the widow of a minor official. They were a miserable couple, but could not separate themselves. She was the model for Lise in *The Brothers Karamzov*, while Dmitri Karamazov is somewhat like the young Dostoyevsky. Three years after his marriage, he was pardoned by the Czar and allowed to return to St. Petersburg. He picked up his literary efforts after a nine-year lapse.

OH, JUST SHOOT ME.

At this point his epilepsy began to take hold. He became enmired in a gambling habit and sank into financial desperation. From this time on, he was always in debt and under pressure to turn in manuscripts for serialization. During the next few years he wrote journalistic pieces, short stories and produced his first full-length novels, *The House of the Dead*, which was drawn from his prison experiences and *The Insulted and the Injured*. When he was forty-five, his wife died. His health was bad and his debts had reached the point where he faced a second prison term. He signed a desperate deal with a cutthroat publisher through which he would lose everything if he did not turn in a novel by a deadline, and it was looking like he was not going to be able to produce it.

At that moment he met Anna, an eighteen-year-old who happened to have been named after the heroine of his unfinished *Nyetochka Nyezvanova*. She knew shorthand and could take rapid dictation. She worked with Dostoyevsky on *The Gambler* and in three weeks it was delivered and he was saved. Anna was the angel that saved his life, and saved Dostoyevsky's work for the world. They were married and so began the period of his life that was to produce his truly monumental work. She was no great beauty, nor was she wealthy or greatly gifted, but she was heaven-sent for him. Besides her dictation talents, she was devoted to him, recognized his genius, understood his creative demon and helped to shield him from his torments. She put up with his excesses, provided him a home,

bore him children and made it possible for the world to appreciate his genius.

Existential Fiction

Dostoyevsky's novels resound with existential themes, which receive uniquely vivid portrayal through the drama set up through the plots. In *Crime and Punishment*, the main character Raskolnikov plots the robbery and murder of an old woman, a pawnbroker whom he feels is of no value to the world. He justifies the crime as a way to save his sister from a loveless marriage to a detestable man in order to save his family from destitution. He believes the thesis that the extraordinary man, like Hegel's "world historical man", has the right to overstep the bounds that apply to the ordinary man. In fact, he reasons, it is only by taking extreme action that one becomes such a superior being. But when he goes through with his plan, and encounters the actuality of murder, his logic and preconceptions shatter and leave him face to face with the reality of what he has done. He is destroyed by his own crime.

Later he realizes his error and confesses it to his new friend Sonia. "I divined then ... that power is only vouchsafed to the man who dares to stoop and pick it up. There is only one thing, one thing needful: one has only to dare. Then for the first time in my life an idea took shape in my mind which no one had ever thought of before me, no one. I saw clear as daylight how strange it is that not a single person living in this mad world has had the daring to go straight for it all and send it flying to the devil! I ... I wanted to have the daring ... and I killed her."

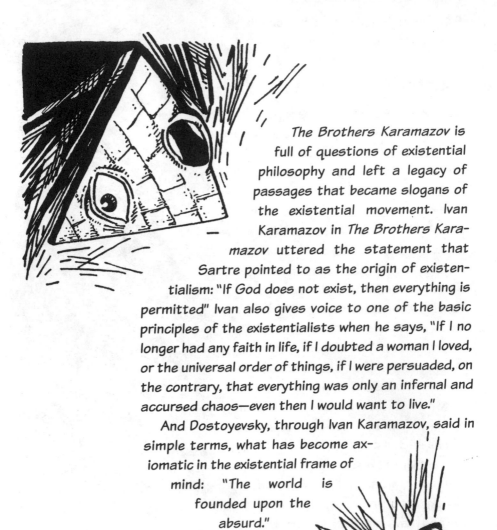

The Brothers Karamazov is full of questions of existential philosophy and left a legacy of passages that became slogans of the existential movement. Ivan Karamazov in *The Brothers Karamazov* uttered the statement that Sartre pointed to as the origin of existentialism: "If God does not exist, then everything is permitted" Ivan also gives voice to one of the basic principles of the existentialists when he says, "If I no longer had any faith in life, if I doubted a woman I loved, or the universal order of things, if I were persuaded, on the contrary, that everything was only an infernal and accursed chaos—even then I would want to live."

And Dostoyevsky, through Ivan Karamazov, said in simple terms, what has become axiomatic in the existential frame of mind: "The world is founded upon the absurd."

Wanted Dead or Alive: God

Dostoyevsky also dealt with the existential theme: Is God dead? Throughout his books he wrangled with the fundamental existential questions about God during the period when religion had seized to rule over human life. It was the period of transition from a religious world view to a scientific one, a transition that was never fully completed down to the twenty-first century.

In a scene of In *The Idiot*, a character named Ippolit, who is given only weeks to live, describes his feelings while looking at a painting of Jesus taken down from the cross. Dostoyevsky was referring to a real painting of Hans Holbein the Younger, not the typically idealized picture of Christ, but an unusually realistic portrayal of what someone might really have looked like after hours of torture. As Dostoyevsky did in real life, Ippolit stares and the painting a long time and wonders if the power that rules the universe is fundamentally malign, heartless, greater even than God.

Speaking through Ippolit, Dostoyevsky says, "One cannot help being struck with the idea that if death is so horrible and if the laws of nature are so powerful, then how can they be overcome? How can they be overcome when even He did not conquer them, He who overcame nature during His lifetime and whom nature obeyed, who said *talitha cumi!* and the damsel arose, who cried Lazarus come forth! and the dead man came forth? Looking at that picture, you get the impression of nature as some enormous, implacable, and dumb beast, or, to put it more correctly, much more correctly, though it may seem strange, as some huge engine of the latest design, which has senselessly seized, cut to pieces, and swallowed up—impassively and unfeelingly—a great and priceless Being, a Being worth the whole of nature and all its laws, worth the entire earth, which was perhaps created solely for the coming of that Being! The picture seems to give the expression to the idea of a dark, insolent and senselessly eternal power to which everything is subordinated..."

Dostoyevsky's work has had an enormous affect on a broad spectrum of culture. And he also deserves credit as one of the definitive voices of the existential movement. Though coming at the beginning of the period, Dostoyevsky dealt with the themes of existentialism thoroughly and definitively. He really laid it down.

The effect of Dostoyevsky on Nietzsche was powerful. Nietzsche discovered Dostoyevsky's *Notes from Underground* by chance in a bookstore, just after it had been translated into French. "The instinct of kinship (or how should I name it?) spoke up immediately; my joy was extraordinary," he said. He called it "a piece of music, very strange, very un-Germanic music."

Soren Kierkegaard

(1813-1855)

Soren Kierkegaard is generally acknowledged as the founder of existentialism, primarily because of his focus on the individual, the existential subject. While Kant and Hegel sought science and objectivity, Kierkegaard emphasized the importance of the individual over the "collective idea" and the philosophical system.

Kierkegaard outlined the main issues that became the basis of existential philosophy. Besides being seen as the father of existentialism, Kierkegaard is also seen as an important precursor to the modernist and postmodernist movements.

Kierkegaard possessed a penetrating intellect and was a prodigious writer who left 18,000 pages of journals when he died at age forty-two, as well as some thirty published works, which spanned many categories, including theology, philosophy, devotional literature, psychology, literary criticism, and fiction. He had a gift for lyricism, a powerful grasp of dialectical logic, was extremely learned and wrote feverishly, his mind on fire with insight and inspiration as if possessed.

The man who is considered the founder of existentialism thought of himself as a religious writer and anti-philosopher. He carried on a raging campaign against the prevailing belief systems of his time: the established church and western philosophy as represented by its leading figure at the time, Hegel.

What I Must Do

The dominant church of his time and place, the Lutheran church, had lost the soul of religion, he said. And he ridiculed ivory tower philosophical reflections and strived to refocus philosophy on the problems of real living people. His main concern was how to live out his own destiny authentically, which for him meant being a Christian.

"What I really need is to get clear about what I must do, not what I must know, except insofar as knowledge must precede every act," he wrote in his journal. "The crucial thing is to find a truth which is truth for me, and to find the idea for which I am willing to live and die. Of what use would it be to me to discover a so-called objective truth, to work through the philosophical systems so that I could, if asked, make critical judgments about them, could point out the fallacies in each system; of what use would it be to me to be able to develop a theory of the state . . . and constructing a world I did not live in but merely held up for others to see; of what use would it be to me to be able to formulate the meaning of Christianity . . . if it had no deeper meaning for me and for my life?"

While Kierkegaard was concerned with what it meant to be a Christian, his ideas have influenced many who do not share his particular religious beliefs because his underlying issues were truth, honesty, authenticity, human destiny and the problems of human existence that are universal.

The Seventh Son

Soren was the seventh child of Michael Pederson Kierkegaard, a peasant shepherd, born in dire poverty, who was able to establish himself in Copenhagen, Denmark, as a successful wool merchant and retire at age forty. He was a morose man who carried a load of guilt for having cursed God when he was young and poor, and perhaps some other things. After he sold his hosiery business, he dedicated himself to theology.

Michael's first wife died childless after two years of marriage. He married his housekeeper, already several months pregnant, who became the mother of all seven children. Soren's father was fifty-six when he was born.

Soren inherited his father's melancholy temperament. "I was already an old man when I was born," he wrote, "but it was granted to me to hide my melancholy under an apparent cheerfulness and *joie de vivre*." He was, he said, "delicate, slender and weak, deprived of almost every condition for holding my own with other boys," but "one thing I had: an eminently shrewd wit, given me presumably in order that I might not be defenseless." He prayed constantly to God to give him the "zeal and patience for the work He Himself would point out for me....So I became an author."

In 1831 he entered the University of Copenhagen as a theology student, according to his father's wishes, but devoted a much of his time to literary, philosophical and historical studies. He spent ten years at the university, living a bohemian life in various degrees of dissipation. He contracted heavy debts, was frequently drunk and at times contemplated suicide.

"I have just now come from a party," he wrote in his journal, "where I was its life and soul. Witticisms streamed from my lips, everyone laughed and admired me, but I went away—yes, the dash should be as long as the radius of the earth's orbit———————and wanted to shoot myself."

He began his career, he wrote, as a "drawing room hero," famous for his "dandyism," and his intellectual bearing. His commanding wit won him admirers as well as enemies. During his student years he cultivated the aesthetic part of his personality, expressing his artistic impulses in his journals and in his first published work.

When he was twenty-seven he became engaged to Regina Olsen, who was then eighteen. He was immediately seized with misgivings and feared that his marriage plans were just an attempt to escape his true calling, a strictly religious vocation. When he tried to break off the engagement, Regina pleaded with him in the name of his father's memory and Jesus Christ, saying she would die if he rejected her. Kierkegaard then felt duty bound, unless she herself made the decision to end the engagement. In order to make that happen, he posed as a treacherous beast, creating scandal in Copenhagen, where Regina's father was State Councillor of the Ministry of Finance. Regina understood and forgave him, then let him go and went on to marry a man who was later appointed governor of Danish West Indies in 1855, the year of Kierkegaard's death.

YOU EXPECTED WILDE?

After breaking off his engagement, Kierkegaard went to Berlin for six months, then returned and produced a tremendous amount of writing. In 1843 he published *Either/Or* under a pseudonym. A few months later he published *Edifying Discourses* under his own name. Before the end of the year, he had published *Fear and Trembling* and *The Concept of Dread*, both under pseudonyms. He published *Philosophic Fragments* in 1844 and *Concluding Unscientific Postscript*, a sequel to it, in 1846.

Shortly before his death Michael Pederson Kierkegaard paid his son's debts and provided him an allowance so that he could live and work independently. Soren found himself in possession of a fortune. He enjoyed living luxuriously, and he gave generously to the poor. His assets dwindled until at the time of his own death there was barely enough to handle the funeral expenses.

His philosophical legacy

Kierkegaard's rebellion focused on what he called "Christendom," the prevailing insititution of Christianity, which to him was an empty social institution devoid of spiritual meaning, and the idealistic philosophy of Hegel.

Idealism, he felt, had become so detached from life that it had become meaningless. He used his nimble wit to ridicule the idealistic philosophers and their "world-historical absent mindedness." People had become so abstracted from life, he said, that they were like the Copenhagen bookseller who had become so absent minded that he barely knew he was alive until one morning he woke up to find that he was dead.

The "systematizers" like Hegel, he said, "are like a man who builds an enormous castle and lives in a shack close by. They do not live in their enormous systematic buildings." Kierkegaard observed that the faculty of the intellect needed to be balanced with more fundamental realities. "It was intelligence and nothing else that had to be opposed," he said. "Presumably that is why I, who had the job, was armed with an immense intelligence." Kierkegaard was not buying the Hegelian system, in which the existing individual was only an insignificant atom in a world historical progression to completion and perfection.

Is The World a Rational System?

To Hegel's dictum that "the real is the rational and the rational is the real," Kierkegaard said, if there were a rational system that could explain the world it would take God himself to construct it or comprehend it, not Hegel. "An existential system is impossible," he said. No mortal human being could create a system that made sense out of everything and resolved all the conflict and chaos of the world, as Hegel had attempted to do. There could never be a completed system to define existence because the world and people in it are always in a state of becoming. Once the system had been completed, the world would have moved on. It never stops moving. No system can sum up life with finality because finality is death. Therefore, instead of systems which we can set on the shelf and admire in their perfection, we must instead seek a "persistent striving for truth."

"As soon as it is remembered that philosophizing does not consist in addressing fantastic beings in fantastic language, but that those to whom the philosopher addresses himself are human beings, so, that we have not to determine fantastically, *in abstracto*, whether a persistent striving is something lower than the systematic finality, or *vice versa*, but that the question is what existing human beings, in so far as they are existing beings, must be content with; then it will be evident that the ideal of a persistent striving is the only view of life that does not carry with it an inevitable disillusionment." (*Concluding Unscientific Postscript*)

Objection to Objectivity

He rejected the philosophers' posture of objectivity, the practice of speaking as though they were outside of the universe looking at it from an imaginary timeless domain like gods and not participants in the world they describe. Speculative philosophers who attempted to contemplate life and the universe as though from outside were ridiculous, argued Kierkegaard. Those who are thinking, no matter who they are, must first exist and therefore can never be outside of life and the universe.

In the idealist view, the detached observer was coolly rational, he did not let his emotions or passions cloud his reasoning. To a rationalist, the only way to think clearly about a subject was to be "disinterested," to have no vested interest in it so that one would not be swayed. In Western philosophy since Plato, only the rational was trustworthy, the senses and the emotions were unreliable.

Kierkegaard felt that Descartes was right to use "I think therefore I am" as the starting point of his philosophy, but wrong, as was Hegel after him, to equate the self with thought only. Existence cannot be contained in thought, it can only be lived. The "I am" portion of the syllogism is much greater than the "I think" portion.

SOMETIMES EXISTENCE LETS ITSELF BE KNOWN WITHOUT A PHILOSOPHICAL ARGUMENT.

The trouble with abstract thought, he said, is that it's *sub specie aeterni*, that is from the standpoint of an absolute spectator. "It ignores the concrete and the temporal, the existential process, the predicament of the existing individual..." he wrote.

"Two ways, in general, are open for an existing individual," Kierkegaard wrote in *Concluding Unscientific Postscript*. "Either he can do his utmost to forget he is an existing individual, by which he becomes a comic figure, since existence has the remarkable trait of compelling an existing individual to exist whether he wills it or not... Or, he can concentrate his entire energy upon the fact that he is an existing individual. It is from this side, in the first instance, that objection must be made to modern philosophy; not that it has a mistaken presupposition, but that it has a comic presupposition, occasioned by its having forgotten, in a sort of world-historical absent-mindedness, what it means to be a human being. Not indeed, what it means to be a human being in general; for this is the sort of thing that one might even induce a speculative philosopher to agree to; but what it means that you and I and he are human beings, each one for himself..."

The Individual

While Hegel's system said that an individual human being was only significant as a passing phase in the dialectic evolution of the World Mind, Kierkegaard rebelled against the submersion of the individual in the mass. He refused to let the individual be reduced to "a paragraph in a system." The professor who teaches such an idea has forgotten what it means to exist. The authentically existing individual will always be infinitely concerned with his own existence and the fulfillment of his own

destiny. The passion of human freedom forces the individual to make choices, and choices involve risk. The existing individual is always in the process of becoming. All earthly life is insecure and that insecurity expresses itself in a striving for truth. Human existence—at an interface between the finite and the infinite, the temporal and the eternal—is constant striving. The Hegelian philosopher forgets that he is too an insecure and striving human being and his explanation of life omits the fact of his own existence.

The only historical fact which I can be absolutely sure of and concerned with is my own existence, he said, and it includes a mix of negative and positive, the eternal and the passing. Its finite limits are what defines its preciousness, its very existence.

When society at large removes the individual human being from its calculations, the results can be monstrous. Kierkegaard urged a return to thinking subjectively, as a living being with the passion of one who is mortal, whose own life is tied up with what he is thinking about.

To correct what he saw as the error in the course of the history of philosophy, Kierkegaard looked back to Socrates, who placed emphasis on philosophic existence, on self-knowledge and self-realization. Kierkegaard praised Socrates as one whose own existence fully exemplified his ideas of goodness and truth. Nietzsche and Heidegger would later fault Socrates for his rationalism and prefer earlier Greeks, like Heraclitus.

Philosophy flowered in Greece with Thales, Heraclitus, and Parmenides, then came to its apex with Socrates, Plato and Aristotle. Heraclitus and Parmenides had their day around 480 BC Socrates was executed in 399 BC for an act of reason that the elders thought destroyed gods of the tribe. Parmenides and Heraclitus were visionaries. Parmenides wrote in verse. Heraclitus wrote aphorisms that were meant to be taken as visionary disclosures of the greater realities. He said such things as: "It is not possible to step twice into the same river. It is impossible to touch the same mortal substance twice, but through the rapidity of change"; "We must not act and speak like men asleep"; "The fairest universe is but a dust-heap piled up at random"; and "If one does not hope, one will not find the unhoped-for, since there is no trail leading to it and no path."

Heraclitus' sayings spoke of universal flow, the continual newness of all things, the dynamism of the "ever-living Fire" of which the universe is made, the harmony of opposites and the importance of being really present and awake, of speaking earnestly and listening intently.

Heraclitus was a philosopher in the mold of the wise men of previous eras, the sages, shamans, readers of signs and dreams, the poets who gave expression to the dreams of the tribe, and articulated its deepest wisdom. He represents the last of the pre-Socratic thinkers. With Socrates, whose work was continued by Plato and Aristotle, came the rise of reason, leading to the separation of mind from spirit and body, and the sobriety and detachment of rationality and science. Although it was a great step forward for mankind, putting great power into the hands of men, it came with a price. The separation of man from his environment, of thought from feeling, was also in a sense the loss of the whole, integrated man.

Nietzsche felt kinship with Heraclitus and was consciously influenced by him. Neitzsche adopted Heraclitus' aphoristic style of writing, appreciated Heraclitus' concept of polemos, as in "struggle" as the "father of all," and even said that his *Thus Spake Zarathustrua* might have been written by Heraclitus.

Heidegger turned to the pre-Socratic Greeks to find the authentic beginnings of Western philosophizing, especially the relationship between being and knowing and between being and thinking. Heidegger believed the insights of Heraclitus and Parmenides were almost immediately lost to mankind in the tidal wave of rationality brought by Socrates, Plato, and Aristotle. He called the subsequent history of Western philosophy, "the forgetting of being" and the rise of thinking that is calculative rather than existential. He wanted to go back and recover that which was lost.

Only when philosophers gained self-knowledge and self-realization, when they became philosophers in an *existential* sense instead of a professional sense, when they *lived* their philosophies and became lovers of wisdom in the manner of Socrates, would their insights be of any value to their fellow man.

Truth is Subjectivity

"Existential truth" for Kierkegaard is that which is lived and not merely thought, the translation of the abstract into the concrete, the ethical and religious appropriation of the ideal, active practice and realization rather than doctrinal knowledge.

How can a thing that is in the process of creating itself know what its completed form is to be? No one can know his place, no one can have his duty proven to him, but must make choices.

Kierkegaard put it this way: the problem of death, understood in an objective, historical sense has only a vague meaning to me, but the problem of my own death concerns me greatly and cannot be dismissed. Knowledge of Hegelian philosophy and universal history will not bring an individual human being one inch closer to coming to grips with his own life and death. On the other hand, reflection on one's own death and the problems of being mortal may help one to learn to think "existentially," that is, to think with the consciousness of the fact that one is an existing, mortal individual, not a disembodied mental process. This is very different from the thinking of the speculative philosopher who writes about what he has never done and never intends to do. In existential thinking, my soul is on trial.

Truth is subjectivity, Kierkegaard said. Everything one does, including searching for objective truth, gets its value from the way it is willed and decided by oneself. Objective truth is easy to understand, two plus two equals four. One's own truth is more elusive. St. Thomas Aquinas had said truth was in the intellect. But Kierkegaard argued that religious truth is not in what one reasons about it, but in how one lives it. A lover is not one who has read a great deal about love, or thought about it, but one who loves, he said. Truth is not just the truth of the intellect, but the truth of the whole person.

Objective truths can be verified by outside sources, facts. They are "existentially neutral" because their truth or falsehood does not change the kind of being you are. Subjective truths, on the other hand, cannot be verified by an outside source. And yet they are things that can change you. Spiritual realities cannot be proven.

Kierkegaard maintained that God is not discovered by abstract demonstration. Religion is a matter of inward choice and requires a leap of faith. Religion in this sense is not the conventional system of habits centered around going to a church, practicing rituals and reciting dogma, but rather the ultimate spiritual quest, the search for spiritual reality, the striving for attainment of spiritual fulfillment, whatever that may be in its ultimate sense. What are we doing here? What is life? What must we try to achieve in our short span of time?

The truth is an individual matter, not a collective one. "A crowd in its very concept is untruth," he wrote, "by reason of the fact that it renders the individual completely impenitent and irresponsible, or at least weakens his sense of responsibility by reducing it to a fraction.... For 'crowd' is an abstraction and has no hands; but each individual has ordinarily two hands...."

The course of science worried him, the way it tried to understand man as a statistic or to explain the whole person in terms of physiological processes, as if that were all there is to it.

"May it not be that the appearance of these fabulous pure thinkers is a sign that some misfortune threatens humanity, as for instance the loss of the ethical and the religious?" he asked. Abstract speculation in the manner of Descartes and Hegel have led to an impoverishment of life. It is a game which can be played in an ivory tower of the academy, but it cannot so easily be applied to real life, where formidable obstacles are constantly appearing. Its result is the "dissolute, pantheistic contempt for the individual man."

Abraham and the Teleological Suspension of the Ethical

He begins *Fear and Trembling* with the Biblical story of Abraham, who almost sacrificed his beloved son at the command of an angel. Abraham becomes for Kierkegaard the "father of faith" who believes in the "virtue of the absurd." Very much concerned with his own choice to break his engagement to Regina, he saw Abraham as an example of one who suspended the ethics of the society he lived in to pursue a higher, more spiritually grounded truth.

He observed three "stages along life's way": the aesthetic, the ethical and the religious. The aesthete is like a tiny child, living for the pleasure or pain of the moment. In the mature person, such an approach to life must collapse into despair. Life has too many problems along the way to be able to sustain oneself just on the pleasurable moments, and the aesthete, the Don Juan, becomes more and more desperate in search of them. The intellectual who looks at things with detachment and the philosopher who imagines himself an observer outside of time and existence are both fundamentally on the aesthetic level. This attitude can only partially accommodate life.

The next level is the ethical. This includes the aesthetic level, but goes on to add something more. When the aesthete chooses himself and his life consciously in the face of the certainty of his own death, he has entered the realm of the ethical. On the ethical level, one concerns himself with more than his own immediate pleasure or pain. But Kierkegaard's brand of ethics is not the abstract speculation on the concepts of good and bad and what to assign to what category in a general sense. He was concerned instead about the choices we must make to bring good or evil into our own lives.

The leap from the ethical to the religious happens when one encounters a situation which goes beyond ethical rules which are considered to be universal for all people in all circumstances. When one must break with the rules that are accepted in the society in which one lives in order to achieve something that may go beyond the norm, but which is true to one's inner calling, he has entered the level of life Kierkegaard calls the religious.

The story of Abraham presents the problem in extreme terms. For a person to kill his own son goes against the values that we hold most deeply as a society.

The story of Abraham loses some meaning in a secular society that no longer believes in angels, but modern parallels still exist. Although a person believes in the moral code that says thou shalt not kill, if some one threatens the life of that person's child, he or she may suspend the customary ethical standard.

A universal moral code cannot always be valid in an individual life because the terms of language and logic in which it is expressed are not sufficient to accommodate all the circumstances that life, in its constant movement and variety, presents. So the ethical person must at times transgress the ethics which he essentially believes in order to remain true to his conscience. When the standard, logical code is not sufficient for a particular situation, guidance cannot come from outside, one must make a choice, an existential leap, and take a risk.

Ultimately, in Kierkegaard's view, the individual is higher than the universal. That is the true ground of existence. There are no universal people, only individuals. And all universal ideas come from individuals.

The person who has achieved the religious level of existence does not reject ethics with disdain. He is essentially moral, so it is in fear and trembling that he makes a decision in certain moments to transgress the accepted code. This is what separates him from the merely amoral person who places himself outside of ethics.

In *The Sickness Unto Death*, which he considered his greatest religious work, Kierkegaard argues that the disciplined spiritual life is more necessary in the modern age than ever before. Re-introducing Christianity into Christendom is more difficult than introducing it into paganism because it requires overcoming the illusion that all who live in Christendom are really Christians. The sickness unto death is despair, which is part of the human condition, of being mortal, a creature bound by earthly conditions yet striving for the eternal and sublime. We struggle for distractions, anything to pull us out of ourselves so we won't feel our despair. But nothing short of religious transcendence will work.

Friedrich Nietzsche

(*October 15, 1844–August 25, 1900*)

Behold the Man!

"Oh thou proud European of the nineteenth century, art thou not mad? Thy knowledge does not complete Nature, it only kills thine own nature... Thou climbest toward heaven on the sunbeams of thy knowledge—but also down toward chaos. Thy manner of going is fatal to thee; the ground slips from under thy feet into the dark unknown; thy life has not stay but spiders' webs torn asunder by every new stroke of thy knowledge."
　　—Nietzsche
　　　Thoughts out of Season, II:
　　　The Use and Abuse of History

Nietzsche is the soul of existentialism, the great probing spirit who led the quest from the dislocation of western civilization ripped from its religious root system toward a new level of spiritual redemption.

　　As with most of those called existentialists, it's debatable whether he really should even be included in the category, or any category. He stands beyond the category of existentialist, even beyond the category of philosophy. His thinking and writing influenced a broad range of fields, including psychology, literature, spirituality, art, music... Even the Nazis appropriated some of his ideas and twisted them to their own purposes. But his defining feature, his most passionate commitment was to the individual in opposition to the herd.

Like Kierkegaard he was a towering intellect, with prodigious gifts. After Kierkegaard laid down the fundamental questions and problems of existentialism, Nietzsche, without knowing Kierkegaard's work, sounded a common chord, though one with very different accompaniment. If Kierkegaard was existentialism's clarion call, Nietzsche gave it fire.

Nietzsche was a great believer in the potential of human beings to rise to greater heights. He was a flash in the fire, who glowed with blinding heat, then burned out quickly in a tragic end. He was a poet as much as a philosopher, an artist at heart, but more than anything, a lover of life.

"Of all that is written," he wrote in *Schopenhauer as Educator*, "I care only for what is written in blood." Philosophy should not be just about ideas, but about how people really live. He tried to live true to his beliefs, and probed relentlessly for the truth, with no fear for where it might lead, even to perilous realms where the belief systems of western culture were not there to protect and comfort. He was fearless in his search, intensely disciplined in his will to open his eyes fully without fear of what may be seen when the filters of culture are removed. In the end he was an isolated broken man.

Little Friedrich: The Prodigy

He was born in a small village in Bavaria. His father died of a brain hemorrhage when Friedrich was five. He was a sickly youth, with weak eyesight and a delicate stomach, but brilliant and studious. The men on both sides of his family were Lutheran ministers and he grew up in a very pious atmosphere, expecting that he too would become a pastor. While still a boy he studied Greek and Latin, became an accomplished pianist, composed music and wrote plays and poems.

When he was seven, he composed his first melodic fragment and began taking piano lessons. When he was ten he heard Handel's *Messiah* and it inspired him to write his own compositions, starting with sketches on the piano. By the time he was twelve he was playing Beethoven sonatas, reading Haydn orchestral scores, composing piano pieces. When he was fourteen he was writing for choir and orchestra. His friend Carl von Gersdorff said, "I don't think Beethoven could improvise more movingly than Nietzsche."

He entered the University of Bonn in 1864 as a theology student to please his mother, but spent more time studying philology. Many of his fellow students were attracted to the idealism of Fichte, Schelling and Hegel; others were followers of the materialism of Vogt, Buchner and Feuerbach, but neither fashion appealed to Nietzsche. After a semester he became disillusioned with Christianity, lost his faith, dropped his theological studies and concentrated on philology. The next year he enrolled in philology at the University of Leipzig.

YEEHAW! I'M DIVIN' RIGHT IN.

The Eggshell Cracks

While in Leipzig, he discovered by accident at a used bookstore Arthur Schopenhauer's *The World as Will and Idea*. After reading a little in the store, he bought it. Here was finally a philosopher who captured his imagination, whose vitality was a match for his own thirst for life. Schopenhauer became his spiritual father and inspired him to expand beyond philology and to continue his studies. Schopenhauer suggested a possibility of salvation without a saviour, that a person could raise himself above the banality and absurdity of existence by his own inner strength. He was also attracted by Schopenhauer's atheism. Christianity, he said, was "lying on its death bed." Unknowingly echoing Kierkegaard, he said, "We are witnessing the euthanasia of Christianity."

In 1867 he signed up for a year of obligatory military service and became part of an artillery unit, despite his poor eyesight. He soon found that his literary bent was unsuited to the life of a soldier and lost his enthusiasm for the military. A fall from a horse in 1868 ended his military career. He returned to the University of Leipzig. While he was there, he was introduced to the composer Richard Wagner, whom he greatly admired. A common appreciation of Schopenhauer was the starting point of their friendship.

Nietzsche became professor of Classical Philology at the University of Basel at the age of twenty-four, an extremely young age for such a post in the German academic community at the time. The University of Leipzig rushed to give him his doctorate without the usual tests.

When he arrived in Basel he renounced his Prussian citizenship and remained stateless for the rest of his life. After one year at Basel, he took leave to join the German ambulance corps and helped wounded soldiers in the Franco-Prussian War of 1870-1871. As a medical orderly, he saw much of the worst of war. He contracted diphtheria, dysentery, and possibly syphilis, according to speculation by Walter Kauffmann. After a year, his health failed and he returned to the university.

As an alternative to Christianity, he was attracted to the symbol of the Greek god Dionysus, the patron saint of the Greek tragic festivals, who represented the transcendent perfection of artistic form and creation, but also the debauchery of ecstatic intoxication and wild abandon. He was attracted to the idea of the joining of opposites, the heights of human culture and the depths of instinct and the primitive. It represented a reconciliation of the opposites he felt within himself and within human nature.

He identified with the pagan god and referred to himself as Dionysus in *Ecce Homo*. He tried to frame a conflict with Dionysus and Christ, but in the end the symbol of Christ of his formative years was resurgent in his life. After his breakdown, when the unconscious had broken free of the bonds of the intellect, he signed himself in letters as "The Crucified One."

Dionysus and Me

In his first major work in 1871, *The Birth of Tragedy from the Spirit of Music,* he wrote that Greek tragedy grew from the ritualistic choral dances of the Dionysus cult. He borrowed Schopenhauer's distinction between the "plastic arts" of architecture, painting and sculpture, which he calls Apollonian, and music, which he calls Dionysian. The Apollonian arts relieve mankind from the harshness of reality by turning its objects into timeless and pleasing forms. The Dionysian arts transmit an intoxicating enthusiasm which defies and transcends the narrowness of ordinary life. Dionysian art is not subject to principles of beauty and not concerned with creating pleasant forms.

It's a more primordial expression of the pain and the passion of life. Nietzsche hypothesizes that the ecstatic choral dance gave birth to the tragic mythos, which in turn took form on stage as a tragic play. The form of tragedy blended the two tendencies by putting the Dionysian ecstasy into a solidified Apollonian form and language. Modern opera, he said, also grows from the Dionysian ecstasy and the modern listener misunderstands it when he thinks the text is primary. The opposite was true with Greek tragedy, he says, with music as the dominant element and the words only a medium to convey the musical mood.

NOW TRAGEDY I CAN DO.

From both Schopenhauer and Martin Luther, Nietzsche adopted the idea of the prevalence of pain, suffering and evil in human life. Luther said that human nature was hopelessly perverted and corrupted by original sin. Though Nietzsche rejected the idea of original sin, he still held to the conviction that human nature is depraved. His philosophy attempted to answer the need for redemption. The Christian idea of redemption no longer reverberated for him, but Schopenhauer's idea did, to a point. The purpose of tragedy was to portray the "nameless pain and grief of mankind, the triumph of iniquity, the mocking dominion of chance, and the irretrievable fall of the just and the innocent..." Tragedy depicts the absurdity of life and the hero in his destruction overcomes the "will to live" and reaches a timeless reality which lies beyond life's contingencies. For Schopenhauer, man could escape only to the world of ideas. For Nietzsche, the tension of paradox and absurdity could only be overcome through creative activity, which transforms itself into ecstatic rapture. In Dyonysian rapture, he alleged, man becomes one with ultimate reality.

His intensive study did not help his health. He took increasing leaves of absence and in 1879 his health broke down and he had to resign his professorship. The university granted him a pension. He then became what he called "a wanderer and a shadow," traveling all over Europe trying to regain his health. His eyesight deteriorated to the point where he could no longer read books. At the age of forty-five he succumbed to psychosis.

A Dream of Prophecy

A dream he wrote down when he was fifteen years old stayed with him throughout his life and was a prophetic metaphor for his lifetime struggle. In the dream he is walking at night in a gloomy wood. He is terrified by "a piercing shriek from a neighboring lunatic asylum." He meets a hunter whose "features were wild and uncanny." In a valley "surrounded by dense undergrowth," the hunter raises his whistle to his lips and blows "a shrill note" that wakes the boy from his nightmare. In the dream he had been going to Eisleben, the home of Martin Luther, the leader of the Protestant movement. When he meets the hunter, it becomes a question of whether or not to proceed to Eisleben or to go instead to Teutschenthal, which means German Valley. The roads diverge and the dreamer must make the choice whether to follow the road to Christianity or the other road, which leads to the natural world, the primeval soil of paganism.

"In the end one experiences only oneself," he said. The systems of philosophy are only many different forms of personal confession. The thought cannot be separated from the life of the thinker.

The Solitary Seeker

He wrote an autobiography of sorts, one of the strangest autobiographies ever written. Some say he was already insane by the time he wrote it, and there may have been some foreshadowing of the collapse that was to come three years later. Yet even if he was already "insane," his mental powers were as formidable as ever. *Ecce Homo* he called it, "Behold the Man," quoting what Pontius Pilate said to the mob before the execution of Christ. Many found its title arrogant, or blasphemous, and inside the book, the outrageousness of the title is upheld, with chapter titles like "Why I am so wise" and "Why I am so clever."

In *Ecce Homo*, Nietzsche gives a definition of his style of philosophy. "Philosophy, as I have so far understood and lived it, means living voluntarily among ice and high mountains—seeking out everything strange and questionable in existence, everything so far placed under a ban by morality."

His *The Antichrist* was a reaction to an institution which had distorted its original ideas beyond recognition. "...the history of Christianity, beginning with the death on the cross, is the history of a misunderstanding, growing cruder with every step, of an original symbolism," he said. "We know, today our conscience knows, what these uncanny inventions of the priests and the church are really worth, what ends they served in reducing mankind to such a state of self-violation that its sight can arouse nausea: the concepts 'beyond,' 'Last Judgment,' 'immortality of the soul,' and 'soul' itself are instruments of torture, systems of cruelties by virtue of which the priest became master, remained master." There was only one Christian, said Nietzsche, and he died on the cross. The church violates what Christ lived for. Only Christian practice, to live as he lived, would be Christian.

His kinship with Kierkegaard, unknowing on both sides, is almost eerie, and the fact that Kierkegaard considered himself a devout Christian and Nietzsche renounced his faith says more about their similarities than their differences. Both began on religious paths and turned vehemently against the church.

Nietzsche was a visionary who foresaw the twentieth Century crisis of Western civilization. In 1873 he wrote: "The great springtide of barbarism is at our door." Like Schopenhauer, Dostoyevsky and Kierkegaard, he rejected Rousseau's image of the underlying goodness of human nature and saw something fundamentally wrong with it. "Man is something which must be overcome," said *Thus Spake Zarathustra*.

While Kierkegaard railed against organized Christianity in the name of a truer, more personal Christianity, Nietzsche felt that the institution of Christianity had brought about the corruption of man, and that man had to go beyond it. He passionately believed in the full realization of the potential of the individual and in living life to the maximum. He loathed the herd instinct, conformity, mediocrity and the mechanization of society. Nietzsche believed, as did Emerson whom he admired, that "society everywhere is in conspiracy against the manhood of every one of its members."

Live Dangerously

In *Schopenhauer as Educator,* Nietzsche wrote, "At bottom, every human being knows very well that he is in this world just once, as something unique, and that no accident, however strange, will throw together a second time into a unity such a curious and diffuse plurality: he knows it, but hides it like a bad conscience—why? From fear of his neighbor who insists on convention and veils himself with it..."

Throughout his work, and his best claim to be an existentialist was his quest for individuality versus the homogenization of the collective. "Behind the glorification of 'work' and the tireless talk of the 'blessings of work' I find the same thought as behind the praise of impersonal activity for the public benefit: the fear of everything individual," he wrote in *The Gay Science* (also translated as *Joyful Wisdom*). "At bottom, one now feels when confronted with work—and what is invariably meant is relentless industry from early till late—that such work is the best policy, that it keeps everybody in harness and powerfully obstructs the development of reason, of covetousness, of the desire for independence. For it takes up a tremendous amount of nervous energy and takes it away from reflection, brooding, dreaming, worry, love, and hatred; it always sets a small goal before one's eyes and permits easy and regular satisfactions. In that way, a society in which the members continually work hard will have more security: and security is now adored as the supreme goddess."

Nietzche urged throwing it all away. "For, believe me, the secret of the greatest fruitfulness and the greatest enjoyment of existence is: to live dangerously! Build your cities under Vesuvius! Send your ships into uncharted seas! Live at war with your peers and yourselves. Be robbers and conquerors, as long as you cannot be rulers and owners, you lovers of knowledge! Soon the age will be past when you could be satisfied to live like shy deer, hidden in the woods!"

Nietzche's famous line "God is dead" comes from *The Gay Science*. Significantly, the character who has seen the death of God is a madman. He calls out into the marketplace but no one pays any attention. He says, "Do we not now wander through an endless nothingness?" Yet although he refers to his alter ego Zarathustra as "the godless," it is not convincing. He is somehow not quite godless, his gods have only changed form, character and name. At the age of twenty he wrote a poem called "To the Unknown God."

"I must know thee, Unknown One,
Thou who searchest out the depths of my soul,
And bloweth like a storm through my life,
Thou art inconceivable and yet my kinsman!
I must know thee and love thee and even serve thee"

His *Thus Spake Zarathustra* was intended to be a single statement of his philosophy but it was presented in a fictional narrative, like a fable. The historical Zarathustra was the founder of the Persian religion in the eighth century BC. In Nietzsche's story, he is a wise man who comes down from the mountains after ten years of a solitary existence and shares his beliefs with the people he meets. Zarathustra decries those who have tried to make existence "smooth and thinkable."

It is a poetic piece, an artistic expression in which the author allowed himself total freedom from academic restraints. He wrote later that the book came to him in a flash of inspiration that was akin to revelation. The book was originally published in four separate parts and more were planned, then abandoned.

The Will to Power was a book that Nietzsche intended to write, but didn't get around to. His sister compiled many of his notes for the book and put them together herself, so the book that actually appeared was not his book, certainly not what he intended to write, but a collection of fragments of his ideas. They were uncritically arranged. Many had been used before and there were significant changes in them. It has often been judged as a definitive work, though it could not have been. In 1888, he gave up writing it, decided to write a shorter work call *The Revaluation of all Values*. He finished the first of four parts, *The Antichrist*. He went on that year to write *Ecce Homo*, which he completed on Christmas Day, 1888. Two weeks later he broke down, insane. He died two years later.

It is commonly believed that his insanity was an unusual case of general paresis, which would indicate that he had syphilis. Since he led an ascetic life, it is not known for sure where he contracted syphilis, if he did.

Nietzsche's Influence

Nietzsche was a major influence on countless writers and thinkers in many fields, existentialism is only one of them. He is discussed in connection with German poetry, psychoanalysis, literature, Darwin, Spengler, Schopenhauer, Wagner. He is claimed by many in diverse realms and there is much in his rich body of work that can be appropriated for different purposes. His thinking was distorted and used by the Nazis, though their practices were diametrically opposed to his beliefs in more ways than they are similar. His theory of the Superman or the Overman, which was a higher form which humans could aspire to or evolve into, was distorted by the Nazis into a techno-barbarian torturer and oppressor, a symbol of many of the aspects of human history that Nietzsche loathed. The Nazis selected other parts of his work to take out of context and appropriate for their purposes, such as his concept of the Antichrist and his glorification of courage and of living with the altitude of a warrior. But he hated much of what Nazism was to stand for: conformism, suppression of the individual by the crowd. When he broke with Wagner, he wrote, "since Wagner had moved to Germany, he had condescended step by step to everything I despise—even to antisemitism."

NEIN! NAZIS AIN'T NIETZSCHE!

Nietzsche holds a central position in the evolution of existentialism. His work was essential to the work of Jaspers, Heidegger, Sartre, Camus, and many others.

Franz Kafka

(July 3, 1883 – June 3, 1924)

"The world order is based on a lie."
— from "Before the Law," a parable from *The Penal Colony*.

Franz Kafka was born in Prague in 1883, the son of a merchant. Prague was in what was then called Bohemia, and was the capital of the Austro-Hungarian empire, in what is now in what is called the Czech Republic. From the late '30s to the late '80s, Prague was part of Czechoslovakia.

As a teenager Kafka read Spinoza, Darwin, and Nietzsche. From 1901-1906, he attended the university, studying German literature, then law. Between 1906 and 1908, he received a doctorate in law, worked briefly for a law firm, interned in the courts and took a job in an Italian insurance company. In 1908 he took a job with a semi-governmental insurance company where he would remain until his terminal illness forced him to retire in 1922. His writing, which was the true passion of his life, was conducted late into the nights as he burned the midnight oil. He died of tuberculosis in 1924 at the age of forty-one.

During his lifetime he published only a few volumes of prose, including *Meditation* (1913), *The Stoker, a Fragment* (1913) *The Judgment* (1912) *Metamorphosis* (1915) and *The Penal Colony* (1919). His full length novels *The Trial* and *The Castle* were not finished or published during his life. Before his death of tuberculosis in 1924, he sent a note to his friend, novelist Max Brod, to have his work destroyed after his death. Brod didn't do it, saying that Kafka asked him to destroy his work knowing that he would never carry it out. The unfinished works were published in the 1920s in Germany. They disappeared during Nazism, but by then had been translated and were published in Paris, London, and New York.

He is often grouped with the existentialists because his writing embodied some of the basic elements of existentialism, primarily his portrayal of the absurd, in a literary form. Kafka's world is one of the most powerful evocations of the absurdity of man's condition in mass society. He was not a philosopher and he didn't write in the form of a philosophical essay, yet he belongs in the existential tradition, which was born of the arts as much as philosophy. Kafka's writing produces a world uniquely his own, yet universally understandable, an absurd world in which human beings are helplessly trapped in cruel machine-like structures of society.

A Huge Insect

In *The Metamorphosis*, the main character, Gregor Samsa, whose name is a slight alteration of the word "Kafka," wakes one morning, "after unsettling dreams, to find himself transformed into a huge insect." It is one of the most monstrous first sentences in literature and begins one of the most dark and depressing stories ever told. In its cruel absurdity, it sums up Kafka's hatred for the bureaucratic society that held him captive his entire life. What begins as an ultimate horror never redeems itself and there is no relief, no improvement in conditions for Samsa as his hopes dwindle further until his life is finally extinguished.

In *The Trial*, the main character is arrested, but is never told what his crime is. Though he tries to find out what he is charged for, he remains locked in uncertainty, wrestling with his own consciousness of guilt.

Kafka's stories pull the reader irresistibly into a dream, a phantasmagorical world in which everything is constantly transmuting, the ground is constantly shifting, reality is fluid, elusive. And the unreliability of events to assume the familiar logical order or stability is not comforting. He was never a writer by profession. He did not write for money, but only to give life to the world that grew within him, that had such power that it took over whatever life he had left after he had given the bureaucracy his daytime hours.

"I consist of literature and am unable to be anything else," he said. Like Kierkegaard, he was unable to follow through with his engagement and carried great guilt over having spurned his betrothed, Felice Bauer.

His legacy is to have given to us a vision so unique that the adjective "Kafka-esque" has become an enduring part of our vocabulary.

Rainer Maria Rilke

(December 4, 1875 –
December 29, 1926)

I'M KNOCKIN' BUT I CAN'T GET IN.

Rilke is widely considered the greatest German poet after Goethe. Today he is probably remembered most for his popular "Letters to a Young Poet." But more important from the standpoint of existentialism was his only novel, *Notebooks of Malte Laurids Brigge,* which states existential themes like the search for an authentic existence, being true to ones own individuality, and the problem of mortality. The book was an influence on Jean Paul Sartre's *Nausea.* Heidegger, too was influenced by Rilke and wrote a long essay about him.

Rilke was born René Karl Wilhelm Johann Josef Maria Rilke in Prague, Bohemia, then part of the Austro-Hungarian empire, now part of the Czech Republic. His father worked as a railway official after failing in his pursuit of a military career. His mother was from a well-to-do Jewish family who lived in a palace in Prague, where young René spent much of his time while growing up.

His parents pressured him to enter a military academy, though he was more artistically inclined in 1891 after five years he left the school because of illness. He later studied literature, art history, and philosophy at universities in Prague and Munich.

In Munich he fell in love with Lou Andreas-Salome, a widely traveled woman of letters. She had studied under Sigmund Freud and shared her knowledge of Freud's ideas with Rilke. It was under her influence that he changed his name from René to Rainer, which she thought was more masculine. Though she was a married woman, he became intimate with her, traveled on two long trips to Russia with her, meeting Tolstoy on one of them. He continued to be close to her till the end of his life.

In 1901 he married the sculptress Clara Westhoff, whom he met while living in the artists' colony at Worpswede, Germany. A daughter, Ruth, was born that year. In 1902 he went to live in Paris, where he encountered Modernism, became involved with the sculpture of Rodin and the painting of Cézanne. In 1910 he published *The Notebooks of Malte Laurids Brigge*, which draws on his experience in Paris.

Though he wrote much more poetry in his life, such as *Duino Elegies* and *Sonnets to Orpheus*, he only wrote one novel, which was the most important of his works from an existentialist point of view. Heidegger called Rilke "the highest form of thinker" and placed him in the German poetic tradition second only to Freidrich Hölderhin. He died of leukemia in December 1926 in Switzerland.

Rilke's *The Notebooks of Malte Laurids Brigge* poses questions that state baldly some of the essential themes of existentialism. Perhaps more importantly the prose embodies a tone that is existential and modern. The consciousness expressed in the prose, the tone, and the form, as an intimate first-person account, had a powerful influence on Jean Paul Sartre, who adopted a similar form and tone for his first book *Nausea*.

In *The Notebooks of Malte Laurids Brigge*, Rilke sums up the existential problems as succinctly as anyone:

Is it possible that despite our discoveries and advances, despite our culture, religion, and science, we have remained on the surface of life? Is it possible that the whole history of the world has been misunderstood? Is it possible that all these people know, with perfect accuracy, a past that never existed? Is it possible that all realities are nothing to them; that their life is running down, unconnected with anything, like a clock in an empty room?

VOILA VOTRE MORT!

Karl Jaspers

(February 23, 1883 – February 26, 1969)

"My book on the *Psychologie der Weltanschauungen* [*The Psychology of World Views*, 1919] appears in historical retrospect as the earliest writing in the later so-called modern existentialism," wrote Karl Jaspers.

Jaspers' claim to have produced the first work of modern existentialism carries some weight. Jaspers brought the work of Kierkegaard and Nietzsche together and created the platform for twentieth century existentialism, what he called *Existenzphilosophie*, or philosophy of existence. With Kierkegaard and Nietzsche, he said, "a new form of reality appears in human history." Much later, when his work was referred to as "existentialism," Jaspers objected to the word because it suggested a school of thought or a doctrine, a position opposed to other positions, and he thought it should be greater than that. "Philosophy can never wish to be less than primordial, eternal philosophy itself."

Jaspers articulated many of the basic themes that were to become known later as existentialism, such as the problem of living authentically as opposed to mundane existence, the struggles of the individual in mass society, the importance of the individual as opposed to the mass, existential freedom and choice, and morality. For Jaspers, the philosophy of being is about becoming.

Lost Generation

Jaspers was a member of the generation that came to maturity as World War I broke, and the war radically affected his way of looking at European civilization. Like the rest of what became known as the Lost Generation, he saw the great optimism and sense of power of the nineteenth century collapse into disorder and futility.

"Quietly, something enormous has happened to the reality of Western man: a destruction of all authority, a radical disillusionment in an overconfident reason, and a dissolution of bonds have made anything, absolutely anything, seem possible," he said in his lecture on "The Origin of the Contemporary Philosophical Situation" (in *Reason and Existenz*). ... "Today, no one can completely and clearly develop the intellectual problems that grow out of such a situation. We live, so to speak, in a seething cauldron of possibilities, but always ready in spite of everything to rise up again."

He was born in Oldenburg, Germany. His father was a jurist; his mother was from a farming family. As a young man, he was interested in philosophy but went into law, following his father. When he realized he didn't care for the law he switched to medicine. He graduated in 1909 and went into clinical psychiatry. In 1913 he got a post as a professor of psychology and ended his psychiatry career. In 1923 he shifted into philosophy. In 1948 he took a post at the University of Basel in Switzerland and stayed there till his death in 1969.

Though he began as a clinical psychologist, he was not a Freudian psychologist. In his first book *Psychopathology* his chief concerns were the individual, and extreme situations. He was also concerned with the problem of method, how it is possible to gather reliable information, and the limits of conceptual knowledge.

As a trained physician, his orientation was scientific. He valued science highly as the only reliable way to establish certain kinds of knowledge. But he was opposed to the misapplication of science in ways that it was not suited, such as to elevate science to the level of a total philosophy or a religion. "...science is invoked to defend something that runs directly counter to the scientific spirit," he said. He called for clarity about science and its limits.

Since science requires choosing premises as starting points, it is guided by philosophy, often unconsciously, in its selection of premises. Its ultimate premises cannot come from the scientific method. For example, it is impossible to prove scientifically that there should be such a thing as science. Science left to itself, he said, becomes homeless. Or as Nicholas of Cusa and many others have said, the intellect is a whore, for it can prostitute itself to anything. Luther called reason a whore. Jonathan Swift in his book *Gulliver's Travels*, refers to a floating island called Laputa, which is believed to represent pure intellect. *La puta* means "the whore."

Understanding the limits of rational processes is essential to using rationality effectively, he said, to being fully rational. "The rational is not thinkable without its other, the nonrational," he said in *Reason and Existenz*. "The only question is, in what form the other appears, how it remains in spite of all, and how it is to be grasped... this non-rational is found in the opacity of the here and now; in matter, it is what is only enveloped, but never consumed by reason. All philosophizing which would like to dissolve Being into pure rationality retains in spite of itself the non-rational; this may be reduced to a residue of indifferent matter, some primordial fact, an impulse, or an accident."

From Kierkegaard he got the notion of *Existenz*, the self that is not an object, but a process, and is more than just consciousness. He defined *Existenz* as true, authentic existence, beyond being an object that just exists, which he referred to as *Dasein*, a word he used very differently from Heidegger's use of the term later. *Dasein*, in Jaspers' terms, is just basic existence, that which is given, little more than the existence of objects. *Existenz*, on the other hand, is attaining that particular human kind of existence which is always living in the space between what is and what is possible. *Dasein* is transitory, but human beings lift themselves above the mere temporal and can strive to attain the eternal. That is transcendence.

He believed that authentic life and even transcendence may be achieved, but is only possible through existential decision and action: the exercise of the freedom to choose. "Existence is real only as freedom ... Freedom is ... the being of existence ... In the act of choice ... in the original spontaneity of my freedom ... I recognize myself for the first time as my own true self... Freedom is the beginning and the end in the process of the illumination of existence."

We arrive in life as if by a leap, he said. But must then make decisions as to what we want to do or be. For Jaspers the *cogito* ("I think") of Descartes becomes *eligo* ("I choose"). I choose therefore I am. In freedom I seize my existence.

Expanding Reason

From Kant he got the idea that reason is not just the rational but an understanding of the limits of rational thought. Kierkegaard and Nietzsche, he said, stretched the limits of what could be thought, staked out the new larger territory of philosophy.

In *Man in the Modern Age*, written in 1930, Jaspers presented existential philosophy as representative of the struggle to attain an authentic existence in the face of the depersonalizing forces of the industrialized world and the drift toward standardized mass society.

He had little use for philosophers in general, but called the outsiders Kierkegaard and Nietzsche, "the original philosophers of the age," not for the specific content of their writings, but because their thinking was not academically inspired, but rooted in existence itself.

A "world-historical" survey of the development of the human spirit like Hegel attempted doesn't give us the ability to deduce what will now happen, he said. "We don't stand outside like a god who can survey the whole at a glance. For us, the present cannot be replaced by some supposed world history out of which our situation and problems would emerge. And this lecture has no intention of surveying the whole, but rather of making the present situation perceptible by reflecting on the past. Nobody knows where man and his thinking are going. Since existence, man, and his world are not at an end, a completed philosophy is as little possible as an anticipation of the whole." [from *Reason and Existenz*]

Jaspers agrees with Kierkegaard that the day of rational metaphysical systems like Hegel's is gone, but focuses his apprehensions not on Kierkegaard's "Christendom" but on the highly organized technological society with its aim to create standardization. Jaspers speaks not of seeking God, but of transcendence. There is no written or historical revelation that can tell us what to do, he said.

Though Kierkegaard and Nietzsche were not recognized for it during their own times, he said, their importance has increased as it became clear that they were the forerunners of the destinies to come. Those destinies were only beginning to dawn in Jaspers time, he said, but they could be outlined by looking at where the work of those two solitary geniuses converged.

The similarities were so great, he said, from the course of their lives down to the details of their thinking, that it makes the differences seem incidental. And it makes their ideas seem to have been "elicited by the necessities of the spiritual situation of their times. With them a great shock occurred to Western philosophizing whose final meaning cannot yet be estimated."

Both questioned reason from the depths of existence, he said. They were not opposed to reason – they were both highly skilled practitioners of reason—but they wanted to expand reason. They wanted to apply all forms of rationality without limit. Both were suspicious of scientific knowledge. They did not believe in the possibility of

ENOUGH WITH ACADEMIA— BUT KEEP BUYING MY BOOKS.

final, all-inclusive systems of philosophy. They saw being as a never-ending interpretation and as something that went beyond thought. Both saw that the nineteenth century had brought a fundamental change to human beings. Both saw themselves as exceptional, as being alone in perceiving the change in their epoch. They were similar in details. Both believed in the meaning of chance events that molded them into what they were. Both used the word "dance" to describe the play of their thoughts and their styles of philosophizing.

Though Jaspers saw Kierkegaard and Nietzsche as having laid the foundation for the philosophy of the time, he did not believe they provided answers to the problems they pointed out. The questions are open. But what they did, was to bring forth "a new type of thought and humanity which was indissolubly connected with a moment of this epoch ... a new total intellectual attitude for men."

Phenomenology

William Dilthey

(*November 19, 1833–October 1, 1911*)

Phenomenology is important to the study of existentialism because it was adopted by Heidegger and later Sartre in their studies of Being. Phenomenology may be seen as a philosophy, but more often it is seen as a method of inquiry, or a way of approaching the subject of philosophy, what one considers facts or the data of experience.

In his inquiry into Being, Heidegger and Sartre after him chose not to follow the scientific method, but the phenomenological method of inquiry, which he adopted from Edmund Husserl. Where the scientific approach tries to make generalizations and predictions through causal formulas and analyses based on scientific logic and the scientific method, the phenomenological approach looks at phenomena from the standpoint of their psychological effect.

This is particularly important when dealing with the study of human beings. Trying to classify human beings into broad categories and making generalizations and predictions about people gives very limited understanding about the nature of one's own existence.

Though one of Hegel's major work was called *The Phenomenology of Mind*, it was William Dilthey who established phenomenology as a separate method or approach to philosophy. Dilthey rejected the idea prevalent at the time that the human sciences should emulate the natural sciences. He separated the kind of knowing of the natural sciences with that appropriate to the human studies such as philosophy, psychology and the social sciences. In the human studies you cannot be an entirely detached observer, because it is through participation that you discover the unique aspects of what it is to be human.

"If we consider man only in terms of perception and knowledge it would be merely a physical fact for us and, as such, could only be explained in terms of the natural sciences. But, insofar as man experiences human states, gives expression to his experience and understands the expressions, mankind becomes the subject of the human studies," said Dilthey. "Life is the fundamental fact which must for the starting point for philosophy."

Edmund Husserl

(April 8, 1859 – April 26, 1938)

Dilthey influenced existentialists such as Karl Jaspers and Martin Buber, but the person who raised phenomenology from an approach to philosophy to a systematic philosophy was Edmund Husserl. In Husserl's Cartesian Meditations goes back to Descartes "I think therefore I am" and declares that you cannot separate the *I think* from what is thought.

Heidegger uses phenomenology as a starting point. Heidegger traced the original Greek root of the word *phenomenon* to mean "that which shows itself." For Husserl, it was to describe what is given to us in experience without preconceptions. Husserl's motto was "to the things themselves," rather than to the preconceptions we usually filter our experiences through. Heidegger was a student of Husserl. Through Heidegger, phenomenology becomes a stream running into existentialism.

AM I THINKING THOUGHTS OR ARE MY THOUGHTS THINKING ME OR ...

An Alternative Method of Knowing

Husserl created a bridge between the thinking and spirit of Nietzsche and Kierkegaard and the earlier Cartesian tradition of logic, and laid the groundwork on which Heidegger and Sartre attempted to build twentieth century existentialism as a systematic philosophy.

Husserl was an exponent of classical rationalism, but he wanted to ground the rationality of mankind on a more solid and comprehensive basis than previous philosophers.

He offered an alternative view to that of positivism and the scientific, objective view. Positivism states that the only valid knowledge is from scientific inquiry, the positive affirmation of theories formulated using the scientific method. But Husserl said that all of our knowledge of so-called objective phenomena is based on subjective experience. Therefore, our subjective experience is really the more fundamental source and ultimately the most reliable.

Husserl said philosophers should cast aside all systems and pre-conceptions that filter their perceptions and look directly at the phenomena themselves, the actual concrete data of experience. "To the things themselves," was the slogan of phenomenology, meaning a return to the sources themselves, casting off all preconceptions and ready-made forms and theories. Philosophy must return to a pure description of what is, Husserl said.

Husserl gave validity to our experience of the world, as distinct from those who asked whether the world was real, or said it is only an outgrowth or creation of the mind, or those who said that the only reliable source of knowledge of the world was through scientific instruments and that the senses and the direct experience cannot be trusted.

Husserl brought a kind of direct realism to philosophizing. That which you see and experience is the real world, he said. His goal was to try to find a point of departure that was pre-systematic, pre-theoretical, something that would underlie different or opposing philosophizing, a common ground of pre-conceptual experience and perception.

Suspending Judgment

Husserl said that the first task of philosophy was to clarify the meaning of what it is to experience the world. Our ordinary experience of the world is a fact among others, a special sort of fact and worthy of careful analysis on its own terms. This gave rise to what he called "bracketing" of experience, a practice in which you suspend judgment of whether your interpretation of your experience is "true," but yet do not impose a theoretical filter over the experience. Instead you just look at both the phenomenon itself as well as at the experience of looking at it. This is easier said than done, but the challenge of attempting it will sharpen the critical faculties.

In phenomenological observation, the observer does not presume the world is just exactly as it may appear or feel, but on the other hand does accept those experiences as a valid part of that world. The observer becomes an observer of his own consciousness in motion.

The sense of anything is not merely present to the mind, but superimposed by the mind on the objects and events which seem to have meaning. The "world" we experience, as a collection of meaningful, organized events depends on the mind to interpret that order.

Martin Heidegger

(September 26, 1889–May 26, 1976)

> "Thinking begins at the point where we have come to know that Reason, glorified for centuries, is the most obstinate adversary of thinking."—Heidegger

Heidegger proposed that Western philosophy had taken a wrong turn way back at Plato (around 400 BC), who had created a misunderstanding of what being itself is by separating the being as a thing from the process of being.

Beginning with the premises of Kierkegaard and Nietzsche that man had become alienated from himself because reason had broken apart from the totality of life, Heidegger set out to redefine thinking itself.

WE WENT WRONG BACK THATAWAY.

Small Town Peasant

Martin Heidegger was born in the German province of Baden in 1889 in a small town, of peasant stock. He was born and raised a Roman Catholic, learned the teachings of Aquinas. His education was initially under the influence of Neo-Kantian thinking, then he came into contact with the phenomenology of Husserl. His employment was as a university professor.

In 1917 he married Elfriede Petri with two ceremonies, one Catholic and another Protestant a week later for her parents. Their first son Jorg was born in 1919, their second son Hermann in 1920, though Hermann was actually the son of Friedel Caesar, which whom Elfriede had an affair. Heidegger had affairs with two of his students, both Jewish, Hannah Arendt and Elisabeth Blochman, both of who he helped to escape the country when the Nazis were killing and imprisoning Jews.

After the war he resumed contact with both of them. Arendt also studied under Karl Jaspers and became an influential writer. She was the author of *The Origins of Totalitarianism* and *Eichmann in Jerusalem*, which grew out of reporting she did for *The New Yorker*. In connection with these studies, she coined the phrase "the banality of evil." After the war she defended Heidegger in the denazification hearings in Germany, though Jaspers spoke against Heidegger in the same forum. Because of the hearings Heidegger was forbidden to teach in Germany from 1945 to 1951, which caused him to gravitate toward the French philosophical community.

Heidegger and the Nazis.

Heidegger became rector of the University of Freiberg in April 1933, about four months after Hitler was appointed chancellor. On May 1st he joined the Nazi party and his inaugural speech ended with three "Heil Hitler"s. In April before Heldegger was appointed rector, Husserl had already been given a leave of absence from the university because he was Jewish and Heidegger cut off contact with Husserl. Under pressure from his publisher, he removed Husserl's name from the dedication at the beginning of *Being and Time*. After the war the dedication was restored to later editions.

As rector, he prevented students from putting up an anti-Semitic poster at the entrance to the university and prohibited a book burning. And his support of the Nazis was typical of philosophy professors at the time in Germany. He resigned the rectorship after only a year, but remained a member of the Nazi party till the end of the war.

In 1945 he wrote an apology for his behavior during his year as rector, which he gave to his son, saying that it had been "an attempt to see something in the movement that had come to power, beyond all its failings and crudeness, that was much more far-reaching and that could perhaps one day bring a concentration on the Germans' Western historical essence. It will in no way be denied that at the time I believed in such possibilities and for that reason renounced the actual vocation of thinking in favor of being effective in an official capacity. In no way will what was caused by my own inadequacy in office be played down. But these points of view do not capture what is essential and what moved me to accept the rectorate."

In an interview with *Der Spiegel* magazine in 1966, he said he had had no alternative but to align himself with the Nazis and his intention had been to keep the university and German science from being politicized. But he also admitted again that he had seen hope in the movement to give Germany a new national consciousness.

SORRY.

Starting Over

IF YOU'RE GOIN' WAY BACK YOU GOTTA LOOK THE PART.

Heidegger began his magnum opus, *Being and Time* (1927) with a quote from Plato: "For manifestly you have long been aware of what you mean when you use the expression 'being.' We, however, who used to think we understood it, have now become perplexed."

He tried to rebuild thought by going all the way back to the foundations of Western philosophy, before the classical Greek philosophy of Socrates, Aristotle and Plato, back to Parmenides and Heraclitus, when philosophy was poetry and poetry was philosophy, before logic was enshrined above the rest of existence. He began at the most elemental block in the foundation of thinking that he could conceive of, the concept of Being itself.

He set out to reopen the inquiry into that most basic concepts by first trying to reawaken an understanding of the meaning of the question, "What is Being?" To the concept of Being Heidegger added the concept of Time, because it was the only way to give form to the concept of Being. Time, he said, was "the possible horizon for any understanding whatsoever of being."

Plato's error, Heidegger said, was that he tried to understand Being as if it were a separate, static thing, almost as if it were an object that could be viewed as though stuck in time. Heidegger instead chose to understand the concept by looking at being as a process, more of a verb than a noun.

Heidegger rejected the scientific method and Platonic logic as his method of inquiry because it lacked the capacity to deal effectively with the element of time, or duration, and because he preferred Husserl's phenomenology as a method of studying the life of human beings.

As we speak

Heidegger liked
to search into
the root meanings
of words, treating them
as cultural artifacts that
embodied within themselves
traces of the history of humankind.
He enjoyed tracing the Greek roots of
words and considered Greek and German the
most expressive languages. He drew great cultural
riches from the exploration of words in his philosophical probes. As was digging into the root meanings of words, he was also developing his own new vocabulary. For the concepts he was trying to articulate, he used words in his own particular way.

Defining *phenomenon* as "that which reveals itself," Heidegger echoed Husserl, saying, "Let the thing speak for itself." The Greek *phainomenon* is also connected to the Greek words *phaos*, or "light," and *apophansis*, meaning "statement" or "speech." The Greek word for truth means the quality of being "unhidden." Truth, he said, is what appears when the veil is drawn away. Truth is not only a quality of logic, but something deeper. A painting can contain a truth, though it is on a pre-verbal, pre-logical plane.

Heidegger traced back to Descartes' doubting of the existence of the external world as the turning point that established the character of modern philosophy. Man was locked within himself and his science told him that the exterior world was not what it appeared to be. He could not even trust that it was really there. But Heidegger said, on the contrary, the most fundamental characteristic of man is that he is "being in the world." He is not separated from the world, but is in it and of it and neither his skin nor any wall can separate him from it. Man is not delineated and defined as being within his skin, but is a *field* of being, of action.

What then is being? Not a being, not anything that is, because anything that is, is a being of some sort, animate or inanimate. But what of being itself? Heidegger defined Being as an event in time and inconceivable outside of time.

Heidegger recognized that the being of humans was different in essential ways from the being of anything else. He distinguished between different meanings of the word "existence". The fundamental existence of an inanimate object Heidegger called "existentia," meaning just existing or being actual, as opposed to not existing. "Existenz," however, in the sense of human existence, means not just that a person is, but that a person is defined by the many possible ways he or she can be.

BUT YOU CAN *TRUST* THE MAN —AND WHAT'S BEHIND THE CURTAIN.

It was Heidegger's contention that Western thought had been preoccupied with the noun form of Being and had practically ignored Being as a verb. For example, the branch of Western philosophy that was concerned with Being was called *ontology*, which translates as the science of the *thing that is*. If it were about the verb form of being, he said, it would have been called *enai-ology*. Philosophy has historically been preoccupied with *things* at the expense of an understanding of the essential movement of all existence.

BEING IS A VERB, BABY!

Being There

Heidegger avoided conventional word usages to force people out of conventional ways of thinking. He used the hyphenated phrase *Da-Sein* to describe an existing human being, the field of existence. *Da-Sein* translates roughly as "being there" or "being-in-the-world," but Heidegger's purpose was to delineate a uniquely human kind of existence.

Da-sein was hyphenated to prevent the tendency to detach the being—the thing—from the background and look at it as if isolated in space and time, which it never really is except in our minds. The word "being" is a participle, a verbal form that can function like a noun. Typically the word "being" is thought of as a noun, a thing, not the verb or what it is *to be*.

Inventing the word *da-sein* gave him a way to avoid the use of words like "man" or "human," which he felt carried the implication that the subject is a thing. It allowed him to avoid the word "consciousness," which returns to the Cartesian dualism, mind as separate from body.

He was trying to free the thought from the Western form of rationalism that put things into a fixed, timeless context, creating an imaginary, ideal world in which the forces of time do not act. When the word "being" is used, it tends to evoke an image that is still, he asserted, a state that is unmoving. This was the tendency of rational thinking that he wanted to correct, to shatter.

Da-sein, being as a verb, was supposed to convey the idea of the process of being, something that is being now, with all that goes with that, in terms of growth, change, decay, aging, damage, destruction, death. All things that exist, he said, exist only in time and can only be understood in terms of time. Classical logical thinking, during which we are not taking into account the reality of time, the motion and effect of time does not reflect the real world we live in.

BEING IS NOW!

The World According to Heidegger

When Being is understood in static terms, it is a dull concept, of little interest to anyone. The broadest generalization you can make about anything is that *it is*. On the contrary, Being as Heidegger conceived it, was a magnificent process, one in which we are all deeply immersed and understand pre-conceptually. It is the field in which our entire world resides. A fish has no concept of water because it is the total medium of its world and no part of his world goes beyond it, so humans understand Being, not as some abstract and remote concept, but as intimately present and all-encompassing. It is of the utmost importance to it.

The field of our existence is intensely personal, not a general thing. According to Heidegger, the "mine-ness" pervades the field. We are in the middle of the world, not separated from it as Descartes may have thought he was. The everyday public part of our lives is "the One," a public persona with which we face the public world, perform our jobs and social functions. It is not the real self which we have the potential of becoming. If we never break beyond this functional role, we are in a "fallen" or inauthentic state of being. Our society—a socially constructed and agreed-upon reality—gives us much which enables us to maintain this illusory state and avoid the confrontation with our real selves, our true potential being. But realities like death and destruction intrude upon that isolated reality and force the realization of our true state upon us.

Heidegger named three categories of existence, or *existentalia*: mood (feeling), understanding, and language.

- Our mood pervades our field of existence. The root of the German word for mood (Stimmung) is connected with the concept of being attuned. We are attuned via our mood. It is our basic mode of being. The fundamental mood is angst, or anxiety. That is the state of apprehending our condition as mortal beings.

- Understanding is not just intellectual understanding but a more basic affinity rooted in existence itself.

- Language is not merely a system of words, spoken or written. Man can use words because he exists in language. When people in conversation fall silent, the silence is part of language too and has meaning because of the primordial attunement of one existing being to another.

We know time, Heidegger said, because we know that we are going to die. Otherwise time would be a mere movement of hands on a clock, signifying nothing. We are not in time, time is in us. For example: The fact that you may die at any time makes it my possibility now, always present. It is the most personal of possibilities because you must do it alone. Only by taking your death into myself can you achieve an authentic existence and stop being the One.

Thrown and Falling

Heidegger marks the beginning of the history of Western civilization with the "fall of being," which occurred when the Greek thinkers detached things from their backgrounds. In Plato's allegory of the cave, the meaning of truth changed from being "unhidden" to being "a correct intellectual judgment." The division of the rational from the rest of being was further deepened with the rise of science and formalized by Descartes.

Heidegger describes man as thrown into an unsympathetic world in which he tries to achieve purposes which ultimately come to naught in death. Man's condition of being, who he is, where he is born, his circumstances are what make up his "facticity." The fact that he finds himself in the world, does not choose to come into the world, is his "thrownness." Man is always "falling" into the world, into the "they," or "the One" ("das Man"), which is the mass, what Kierkegaard referred to as the "crowd" or the "public," and Nietzsche called the "herd," a faceless power that governs us all. It is a shared abstraction and it exerts a force against one's individuality, tends to pull the individual toward mediocrity and averageness.

97

Da-sein exists in tension between his facticity, the given state in which he finds himself, and his possibilities, that to which he may aspire. He is always in a forward thrust toward his possibilities. Heidegger uses the word "care" to characterize the tension between facticity and our possibilities, our authenticity versus our "falling into the world" and the "they." It is the structure of our everyday being-in-the-world. It refers to the multitude of ways our existence impinges on the world around us, all the ways that we use the things in our environment, all the things that connect us to it. Care is our practical concerns, that which holds us in the everyday world.

Da-sein can attain an authentic existence only by breaking away from the "they" and realizing its own possibilities, of which the ultimate one is always death. One becomes inauthentic when it falls back into the "they," identifies itself with its facticity [its earthly circumstances or condition], and behaves as though it will never die. In inauthenticity, or the state of being "fallen," the search for understanding is only idle curiosity, philosophical discourse is only idle talk, thinking is nothing more than calculation.

Only by "being toward death" can one achieve an authentic existence. A full acceptance of death as a possibility in this moment frees one from the impersonal, the social one-among-many, and allows you to become truly himself. Heidegger calls this "freedom toward death" or "resoluteness." This does not mean brooding over death, but including it realistically and consciously as part of your possibilities in every project one undertakes.

The ultimate freedom is taking on a task which is uniquely my own. This is what Heidegger means by "existential decision" or "choice." Heidegger contended that Being had been the central problem of Western philosophy from the Pre-Socratics through Hegel, but after Hegel fell into oblivion and the meaning of Being was taken as something self-evident.

An Unfinished Symphony

Being and Time was intended to be the first part of a theory of being as a whole (ontology). Only the first two sections of what had originally planned to be two main parts with three sections each was published (two out of six). The two sections came to over four hundred pages of fastidious analysis of Da-sein and its temporality, but it was only preparatory to what was to follow, but never did. It was to go on and analyze Time as the horizon of being. It was then to have gone into depth criticizing the studies of being through the history of Western philosophy. Its incompleteness affected how the work was to be understood. What was to be its primary subject, being, was barely treated.

In the intended second part of *Being and Time*, Heidegger was going to try to strip away the modern lens through which he thought Descartes, Kant, and Aristotle were distorted. Then he was going to show the ways he thought their thinking on being was limited. He did write a number of other works in his remaining years, but the final two-thirds of the major work did not happen. The analyses of Aristotle, Kant, and Descartes never appeared, though his book *Kant and the Problem of Metaphysics* was related to the proposed major work. In the later work there was an increasing interest in the relationship between philosophy and poetry. The inter-relation of philosophy and literature, he says, was closest in the ancient Greeks, especially in the pre-Socratics. Poetry for Heidegger is not a mere embellishment of human existence, an aesthetic decoration of culture, but is the deepest "ground of human history."

All existential philosophy draws on the themes outlined and inspired by Kierkegaard and Nietzsche, but much of the conceptual formation and articulation of the existentialists, and much of their vocabulary came from Heidegger. *Being and Time* was the work that most influenced Sartre, Merleau-Ponty, and others who carried the banner of existentialism.

Much of Heidegger's thinking, its terms and its concepts, were appropriated by Sartre, then adapted (some have said "perverted") to suit Sartre's own purposes. Heidegger himself disavowed any association with Sartre and the existentialists. Though he is almost always considered as one of the most important contributors to the philosophy of existentialism, Heidegger preferred to distinguish himself from the tradition and call himself a "philosopher of being." When he saw the direction Sartre had taken his ideas, is said to have exclaimed, "Good God, I never intended that!"

In his late work *Discourse on Thinking* (1959), Heidegger is still trying to redefine thinking. In this work Heidegger said that men were becoming thoughtless. It is only possible that humans could become thoughtless or thought-poor because man "at the core of his being has the capacity to think; has 'spirit and reason' and is destined to think." Man today, he said, is "in flight from thinking" and most of what passes for thinking is a certain kind of thinking: calculation. "Its peculiarity consists in the fact that whenever we plan, research, and organize, we always reckon with conditions that are given. We take them into account with the calculated intention of their serving specific purposes. Thus we can count on definite results. This calculation is the mark of all thinking that plans and investigates. Such thinking remains calculation even if it neither works with numbers, nor uses an adding machine or computer. Calculative thinking computes...Calculative thinking never stops, never collects itself. Calculative thinking is not meditative thinking, not thinking which contemplates the meaning which reigns in everything that is...There are then, two kinds of thinking, each justified and needed in its own way: calculative thinking and meditative thinking." Meditative thinking may not just happen, it may take effort, just as calculative thinking does, but everyone can do it, "Because man is a *thinking*—that is, a *meditating* being. Thus meditative thinking need by no means be 'high-flown.'" It is enough if we dwell on what lies close and meditate on what is closest; upon that which concerns us, each one of us, 'here and now' here, on this patch of home ground; now in the present hour of history."

Though Heidegger did not call his philosophy existentialism, it is an important contribution to existential philosophy, an important statement of many of its fundamental principles.

Remembering Nietzsche's statement that of all philosophy he cared only for what was written in blood, it is hard to divorce the philosophy from the life of the philosopher that produced it. Heidegger stated that the central problem of human beings was the struggle to realize their own individual possibilities in the face of pressure to fall into the anonymity of the "They." This seems to be in diametric opposition to the practices of Nazism, in which individuals were all supposed to sacrifice themselves to the state. Yet the fact remains that Heidegger embraced the Nazi movement, took on its rhetoric and tried to accommodate it to his own philosophy, with strange results indeed.

While Kierkegaard and Nietzsche rocked the world of philosophy with bold, passionate voices from outside the academic community, Heidegger was well-entrenched within the academic world, and his writings are characteristic of that community. *Being and Time* is extremely dense and dwells on microscopic points of definition. And yet his philosophy is such a radical departure from the philosophy that preceded it that it was soundly rejected by much of the more conventional philosophical community.

Even many of the greatest scholars of Heidegger consider him to be at times obscure, perhaps inconsistent or just incorrect. Walter Kaufman said, "Heidegger's difficulty is almost legendary."

Jean Paul Sartre

(June 21, 1905–April 15, 1980)

"Something has happened to me, I can't doubt it anymore. It came as an illness does, not like an ordinary certainty, not like anything evident. It came cunningly, little by little..."

The first sentence in *Nausea*, Jean Paul Sartre's first novel published in 1938, is a good description of how existentialism awakened in the consciousness of Western civilization.

More than anyone else, Sartre is identified with existentialism. Though existentialism draws on a tradition that goes back to Kierkegaard, it was with Sartre in the 1940s that it was named and came to full recognition as a movement. French existentialism was forged in the blast furnace of World War II and the Nazi occupation of France.

When existentialism burst onto the world as a popular international phenomenon, the name and face associated with it were those of Sartre. He was 5 feet 3 inches tall. He drank a lot of whisky, smoked two packs of cigarettes a day and took drugs to stimulate himself when he wrote. He was the one who defined existentialism and acted as its spokesperson. He was its popularizer.

He took up the philosophy of being from Heidegger and Jaspers and the phenomenology of William Dilthey by way of Edmund Husserl and wove them into his own system. He drew on the tradition, developed it into his own philosophy tempered by his experience of war and the Nazi occupation of France, and articulated it for the world. Sartre was the first self-proclaimed existentialist and one of the few philosophers associated with the tradition who ever actually called himself an existentialist. He proudly preached his existentialism to the world.

Sartre was enormously prolific, producing writing in prodigious quantities consistently throughout his life. His output has been calculated as high as twenty published pages for every day of his entire life. He wrote novels, plays, articles, essays and philosophical treatises.

Though he did not coin the term, he embraced it and emerged as a full-fledged existentialist with a lecture he called "Existentialism is a Humanism," which was his explanation of what existentialists stood for. It was a harsh philosophy that required individuals to take complete responsibility for their every action, for what they are, and for their worlds.

He disputed Descartes' statement "I think therefore I am," saying instead that, "existence precedes essence." Before we think, we must first exist. We are "thrown into the

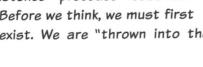

world," and then we make ourselves whatever we become. Man is nothing at birth and throughout is life he is nothing more than his past commitments.

A recurring theme from the beginning of Sartre's fictional work through his major philosophical work is the conflict between oppressive and spiritually-destructive conformity (literally *mauvaise foi*, or "bad faith") and an authentic life. Bad faith is an attempt to escape anguish by pretending that one is not free. To believe in anything outside one's own will is bad faith. Rationality itself can be bad faith when it leads to trying to impose a false sense of order and structure on phenomena that is fundamentally random and irrational.

Echoing Kierkegaard he said "we must begin from the subjective." In a godless world, there is no authority for what is good or bad, right or wrong. The only worthwhile goals are those one sets for himself.

Thrown (Gently) Into Paris

Sartre was born in Paris to an officer of the French navy and a woman of German-Alsatian origin who was a cousin of Nobel Peace Prize winner, Albert Schweitzer. Jean-Paul's father died when he was fifteen months old and he was raised by his mother and other family members, who doted on him. Sartre's mother's father, Charles Schweitzer, was a German professor and taught Jean-Paul mathematics and classical languages when he was young. He was first turned on to philosophy by reading Henri Bergson's *The Immediate Data of Consciousness*.

Sartre began his career as a freelance writer and philosopher in 1924. He studied at the École Normale Supérieure, where he met Simone de Beauvoir, who was to be a lifelong companion and a major writer in her own right. He graduated in 1929, was drafted and spent eighteen months in the French army. From 1931 to 1945 he worked as a secondary school teacher. In between terms he traveled in Egypt, Greece, and Italy. In February 1933 he went to Berlin for a year to study the philosophy of Edmund Husserl and Martin Heidegger at the French Institute. According to de Beauvoir, in September 1935 he took mescaline, the consciousness-altering drug that occurs naturally in peyote cactus.

Sartre said he saw lobsters, orangutans, and houses gnashing their jaws. He reportedly found the experience very disturbing and did not repeat it. But it appears to have had some influence on the writing of his first novel *Nausea*. Many of the scenes carry the distinct feeling of an altered state of consciousness. "I *see* the future. It is there, poised over the street, hardly more dim than the present... I don't know where I am any more, do I see her motions, or do I *foresee* them? I can no longer distinguish present from future and yet it lasts, it happens little by little ... This is time, time laid bare ..."

SHEESH! I'D RATHER TEACH HIGH SCHOOL.

Published in 1938, *Nausea* was a short novel written in the style of a personal journal with an acute focus on present-tense experience. The unconventional narrative style embodies, in a sense, the existential philosophy which Sartre was to later attempt to formulate systematically.

Originally he named the novel *Melancholie* ("melancholia"). But his publisher persuaded him that that *Nausea* would be a stronger title. Though classified as a work of fiction, it differed radically from the fiction of the day. Sartre believed that contemporary novelists, such as Dos Passos, Virginia Woolf, Joyce, Huxley, Gide and Faulkner, all wrote within the philosophical world view of Descartes and Hume. Sartre wanted to write a novel based upon a new world view that had assimilated the philosophy of Heidegger.

While criticized as a novel in terms of standards of conventional plot structures and attitudes, *Nausea* was an explosion, a stylistically unique book that shone with a new kind of consciousness.

In *Nausea* the narrator describes his countrymen with alienation and disdain, and illustrates the kind of thinking existentialism would ultimately try to overthrow, a dull, conventional, mechanical, hypnotized kind of thinking in terms of general categories, statistical facts, a false sense of stability and security and the illusion of timelessness.

"They come out of their offices after their day of work, they look at the houses and the squares with satisfaction, they think it is their city, a good, solid, bourgeois city. They aren't afraid, they feel at home. All they have ever seen is trained water running from taps, light which fills bulbs when you turn on the switch, half-breed bastard trees held up with crutches.

SOME BOOKS YOU DON'T READ IN THE LIBRARY.

NAUSEA

They have proof, a hundred times a day, that everything happens mechanically, that the world obeys fixed, unchangeable laws. In a vacuum all bodies fall at the same rate of speed, the public park is closed at 4 p.m. in winter, at 6 p.m. in summer, lead melts at 335 degrees Centigrade, the last streetcar leaves the Hotel de Ville at 11:05 p.m. They are peaceful, a little morose, they think about Tomorrow, that is to say, simply, a new today; cities have only one day at their disposal and every morning it comes back exactly the same...And all this time, great, vague nature has slipped into their city, it has infiltrated everywhere, in their house, in their office, in themselves. It doesn't move, it stays quietly and they are full of it inside, they breathe it, and they don't see it, they imagine it to be outside, twenty miles from the city..."

Consciousness Reflected

In 1937 he published *Transcendence of the Ego*, in which he took a phenomenological approach to examining consciousness. In it he defines "unreflected consciousness" as thinking without a subject. It is the conventional kind of thinking about things without thinking of ourselves in relation to them.

Reflected consciousness, on the other hand, is thinking that does include ourselves. The "I am" of Descartes' statement: "I think, therefore I am," is only present in reflected consciousness. Sartre disagreed with Descartes that thinking proves the existence of the thinker. On the contrary, consciousness is "an impersonal spontaneity" flowing constantly out of nothing. The purpose of the ego, Sartre speculated, may be to filter the overwhelming flow of consciousness into a narrow stream of reflected consciousness of an individual.

Tempered by War

In September 1939, France and England declared war on Germany in response to the Nazis invasion of Poland and Sartre was again drafted into the army. He was stationed at the front of what was called the "phony war," because for months neither side made a move. From Sartre's trench he could see German soldiers.

At the front he continued his enormously prolific output, filling notebooks with reflections and working out some of the ideas that later emerged in his philosophical writings. Many of the key passages from his major philosophical work *Being and Nothingness*, appeared first in these journals, but in a more natural, accessible language. Turned out in what would seem the most inopportune situation, the journals are some of his richest writing, unhindered by the formal structures of more serious works. Every page shines with Sartre's always-penetrating intelligence, the dazzling dexterity of his intellect reflected upon all he sees or encounters.

The method of Heidegger and such as may come after him is basically the same as that of Descartes: interrogating human nature with methods appertaining to human nature itself; knowing that human nature already defines itself by the interrogation it formulates upon itself. All of a sudden, however, we posit as the object of our interrogation not the mind, not the body, not the psychic, not historicity, not the social or the cultural, but the human condition in its indivisible unity. Idealism's error was to posit the mind first.

AW, VINNIE, YOU'RE MORE FAMOUS FOR DESTROYING YOURSELF THAN FOR YOUR PAINTINGS, MY HERO!

Rather than his creativity being stymied by being shuttled to the front, Sartre told Beauvoir that he found more time to write on the front than in civilian life. And his absorption in writing insulated him from the horrors of war.

In relation to Gaugin, Van Gogh and Rimbaud, I have a distinct inferiority complex because they managed to destroy themselves. Gauguin through his exile, Van Gogh through his madness and Rimbaud most of all, because he managed to give up even writing. I am more and more convinced that, in order to achieve authenticity,

109

something has to snap. This is really the lesson Gide drew from Dostoyevsky, and it's what I shall show in the second book of my novel. But I have protected myself against anything snapping. I have bound myself hand and foot to my desire to write. Even in war I fall on my feet, because I think at once of writing what I feel and what I see.

During his time at the front between fall of 1939 and the next June, he filled fourteen notebooks, nine of which were lost. He also wrote daily to his mother, Beauvoir and Wanda Kosakiewicz – his current heartthrob. And he completed the novel *The Age of Reason* and some shorter works, a total output estimated at a million words.

When the Nazis overran the French forces in June 1940, Sartre was captured and imprisoned in Germany. In 1941, he was released, or escaped, and returned to Paris, where he joined the resistance. He wrote for the resistance publications *Les Lettres Française* and *Combat*. After the war he founded a monthly literary and political review, *Les Temps Modernes (Modern Times)*, named after the Charlie Chaplin film. In the pressure cooker of the brutal Nazi occupation, Sartre's existentialism took form.

Sartre's experience during the degradation and terror of the occupation left an indelible mark on his character and was central to the development of his thinking and writing. For him even war was viewed as an opportunity to develop as a writer. His writings about it are characteristically striking, always a slap in the face. In *The Republic of Silence*, he wrote:

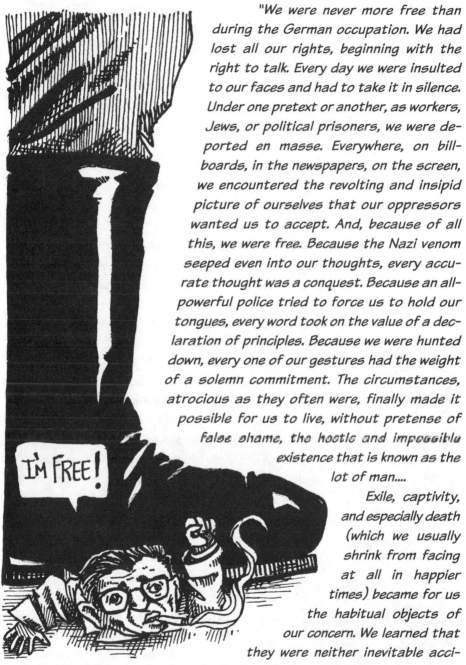

"We were never more free than during the German occupation. We had lost all our rights, beginning with the right to talk. Every day we were insulted to our faces and had to take it in silence. Under one pretext or another, as workers, Jews, or political prisoners, we were deported en masse. Everywhere, on billboards, in the newspapers, on the screen, we encountered the revolting and insipid picture of ourselves that our oppressors wanted us to accept. And, because of all this, we were free. Because the Nazi venom seeped even into our thoughts, every accurate thought was a conquest. Because an all-powerful police tried to force us to hold our tongues, every word took on the value of a declaration of principles. Because we were hunted down, every one of our gestures had the weight of a solemn commitment. The circumstances, atrocious as they often were, finally made it possible for us to live, without pretense of false shame, the hostic and impossible existence that is known as the lot of man....

Exile, captivity, and especially death (which we usually shrink from facing at all in happier times) became for us the habitual objects of our concern. We learned that they were neither inevitable accidents, nor even constant and exterior dangers, but that they must be considered as our lot itself, our destiny, the profound source of our reality as men."

In Sartre's story "The Wall" he describes with microscopic detail the scene inside a prison in which prisoners of war are condemned to death. It is a grim vision, and shocking to read.

"It's like a nightmare," Tom was saying. "You want to think something, you always have the impression that it's all right, that you're going to understand and then it slips, it escapes you and fades away. I tell myself there will be nothing afterwards. But I don't understand what it means. Sometimes I almost can ... and then it fades away and I start thinking about the pains again, bullets, explosions. I'm a materialist, I swear it to you; I'm not going crazy. But I'm the one who sees it, with my eyes. I've got to think... go on for the others. We aren't made to think that, Pablo. Believe me: I've already stayed up a whole night waiting for something. But this isn't the same: this will creep up behind us, Pablo, and we won't be able to prepare for it."...

He certainly talked to keep himself from thinking. He smelled of urine like an old prostate case. Naturally I agreed with him. I could have said everything he said: it isn't natural to die. And since I was going to die, nothing seemed natural to me, not this pile of coal dues, or the bench, or Pedro's ugly face...

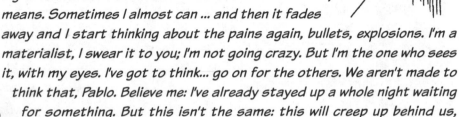

THERE IS REALITY AND THEN THERE IS REALITY

Sartre's brutal frankness about extreme situations brought the criticism that existentialism was morbid. But though the conditions in occupied France were certainly extreme, "out of the ordinary," the events portrayed in Sartre's fiction were representative of real events and not even the worst of what went on during World War II. Though the situations portrayed are extreme, they bring to focus underlying issues of life and death that are present at all times, but are usually more easily ignored.

The Nazi occupation was extreme and squeezed its victims to the limits of their existence. According to Sartre, in the most extreme cases, the only freedom that remained was the freedom to say "No."

I Am Therefore I Think

Stating that freedom was essentially negative was consistent with Descartes, who began his philosophy by negating everything. But Sartre pulled Cartesian doubt out of the ivory tower of ideas and made manifest existentially, in action. Sartre was fundamentally a Cartesian who read Proust and Heidegger, experienced psychedelic drugs, and lived when the cataclysmic disasters prophesied by Kierkegaard, Dostoyevsky and Nietzsche had come to pass. While Descartes was solidly anchored in his Christian faith and relied on God to pull him back to safety after his mental journey through the labyrinth of uncertainty, Sartre was a citizen of the twentieth century for whom God was dead and who already had seen the horrors of western civilization at its worst, with no academic ivory tower to return to for safety.

As most people think in terms of a kind of Platonic reasoning that takes place in an imaginary space in which time or the concerns of a mortal being do not exist, Sartre said that most people really live imaginary lives. In his book *L'imaginaire* (translated to English as *The Psychology of the Imagination* or *The Imaginary*) he defines the fundamental difference between imaginary events and real life.

HE'S GOT A BIBLE— ALL I'VE GOT IS A BLANK SHEET.

"*Proust has shown well this abyss which separates the imaginary from the real; he had made it very evident that one cannot find a way from one to the other and that the real is always accompanied by the collapse of the imaginary, even if there is not any contradiction between them, because the incompatibility comes from their nature and not from their content. It*

113

must be added that, from the very fact of the essential poverty of the images, the imaginary actions which I project have only the consequences which I want to give them. If I strike my enemy in imagination, blood will not flow or, rather, it will flow to the extent that I would like. But in front of the real enemy, in front of this real flesh, I am going to foresee that real blood will flow, and that alone will be enough to stop me. Thus there is a continual gap between the preparation for an action and the action itself. Even if the real situation is almost what I had imagined it to be, it is still true that it is different in nature from my imaginings. I am not surprised by what happens, but by the shift into a different world...Every moment, in contact with reality, our imagining self breaks up and disappears, giving way to the real self. For the real and the imaginary, in essence, cannot co-exist...

From this we may well think that individuals should be placed in two great classes, according to whether they will prefer to lead an imaginary life or a real life..."

Pièce de Résistance

Sartre wrote his major philosophic work *Being and Nothingness* during the occupation and it appeared in 1943. It is a giant work, shining with Sartre's brilliance and mental agility, but uneven. In it, he begins with Heidegger's ideas and takes them in a new direction. Sartre was extremely well-grounded in the philosophy before him. He was a Cartesian who was well versed in the dialectical techniques of Hegel but used them to build an existential rather than an idealistic world view. The result is a philosophy that assimilates and sums up the history of philosophy, but especially resonates with the existential principles established during the preceding century by Kierkegaard, Nietzsche, Jaspers, and Heidegger.

He divided Being into two essential kinds: being-for-itself and being-in-itself. The in-itself, such as a nonliving object, is self-contained. It's just what it is, no more no less in any moment. The for-itself on the other hand exists in the field of consciousness and is therefore always beyond itself, in its past or its future, or in its imaginative flights to the limits of the universe. Human existence is perpetual self-transcendence. We never possess our being as we possess a thing, it is always moving beyond us. This is the fundamental uneasiness, the anxiety of human existence. We seek security, the stability of a thing, but this is not possible as long as we are living. In fact that kind of stability runs counter to that life force that separates us from the inanimate world.

Sartre interweaves ideas of the in-itself and the for-itself to describe the complexities of human psychology. He describes human being in contrast to the nothingness of our existence, like the yin and yang of Taoism, something or nothing, foreground and background. He sees the nothingness of the self as a basis for the will to action. Human existence in an uncaring universe can be given meaning only through the project that one launches out of nothingness.

While the in-itself is complete, the for-itself—human existence—is always striving to fulfill itself, always divided between its present self and a future self. Man strives for the completeness, the calmness of the for-itself, but cannot possibly achieve that and retain his consciousness of self. He strives to unite two forms of being that are mutually exclusive, then tries to overcome the difference by striving to

THE CHAIR I CAN HOLD IT'S MYSELF I CAN'T QUITE GET A GRIP ON.

be divine. This is impossible, so man is "a futile passion," he said. "We are existents who can never catch up with themselves," he said. Man can never attain the fullness of being that he desires, but as a human existent, he must realize himself in action, to storm ahead toward an impossible goal. He is always separated from his past and future selves by the "nothingness" that always intervenes between himself and time. Constantly stymied in his projects and thrown back upon his fragile momentary existence, man experiences dread and anguish. He tries to rid himself of the responsibility of his own existence to forces outside of himself in the environment or religion, but all attempts are essentially dishonest and doomed to failure. Man is what he makes himself and he alone is responsible.

For Sartre, existence is pure contingency, a chance event, simply being there for no comprehensible reason. Postulating God as a first cause does not explain existence, he said. It is up to us to define ourselves. Borrowing from Heidegger and Jaspers, Sartre said human beings, are "thrown into the world" and "condemned to be free." Sartre begins by attacking the idealism of Descartes, though he later returned to his own kind of idealism. For idealists, the entire universe is made up of artifacts of the human mind. In *Nausea*, the center of the world is not human consciousness, but the massive exterior physical universe, which is symbolized in everyday objects, through which a sinister power seems to shine.

The world of idealism is a world without human beings, but in the real world, man exists with others. In love, I approach the other as a subject and present myself as an object, as attractive as I can make it. In sexual desire, I approach the other as an object of which I try to gain possession. In these, or in other kinds of relationships, my own projects may be crossed and paralyzed by the projects of "the other." Therefore, according to Sartre, the natural attitude among human beings is not love, peace and harmony, but hate, conflict, and strife. As he states in his play *No Exit*, "Hell is other people."

"HELL IS OTHER PEOPLE" AND REAL HELL IS WHEN THOSE OTHER PEOPLE WON'T GIVE YOU ANY ATTENTION!

Human beings finally confront the total strangeness of the other in the phenomenon of death, he said. Death cannot be assimilated into human consciousness. One cannot experience or anticipate it. It is the absurd annihilation of the human self. It does not give meaning to life, but only demonstrates its absurdity.

According to Sartre, human beings are radically free to make choices and guide our lives toward our chosen goals or projects. And there is no escape from that freedom. We are utterly and entirely responsible for ourselves. His demand for self responsibility was utterly merciless. The harshest taskmaster, Sartre allowed absolutely no exceptions, as he laid out sternly in *Being and Nothingness*:

"*There are no accidents in life. A community event which suddenly bursts forth and involves me in it does not come from the outside. If I am mobilized in a war, this is my war; it is in my image and I deserve it. I deserve it first because I could always get out of it by suicide or by desertion; these ultimate possibilities are those which must always be present for us when there is a question of envisaging a situation. For lack of getting out of it, I have chosen it. This can be due to inertia, to cowardice in the face of public opinion, or because I prefer certain other values to the value of the refusal to join in the war (the good opinion of my relatives, the honor of my family, etc.) Anyway you look at it, it is a matter of choice.*"

Existence precedes essence in human beings, he explained, because, one exists "before he can be defined by any concept ... First of all man exists, turns up, appears on the scene, and only afterwards defines himself. ... at first he is nothing. Only afterward will he be something, and he himself will have made what he will be. Man is nothing else but what he makes of himself. Such is the first principle of existentialism."

We choose ourselves, Sartre said, we choose what we are to be, though we must choose from the possibilities within situation in which we find ourselves, our facticity. We do not create our facticity, such as where we are born and when, but we do choose it by not negating it. We re-affirm our birth at each moment by not ending our lives. We are free and responsible for ourselves and there is no escaping the responsibility, though we may live in denial of it. Sartre said we are "condemned to be free."

Fading Into History

Sartre is paradoxical in the sense that he tried to build a traditional philosophical system in existentialism, which began with the declaration by Kierkegaard that, "An existential system is impossible." Sartre blends the elements of his predecessors in a new way. In some ways he is a classical philosopher. Though he rebelled against traditional philosophy, he sprung from within it. He was not an outsider to the academy like Kierkegaard.

As the Post War period became the Cold War, Sartre developed politically along Marxist lines, but not along the lines of Stalinist Russia, which became a totalitarian state in many ways comparable to the Nazis and far from the egalitarian Workers State that Marx had described. Sartre stubbornly defended the Soviet state even as evidence surfaced of Stalin's oppression, then finally turned against Stalin, but continued to defend the Soviet state. In 1964 he was awarded the Nobel Prize for literature, but refused to claim it in protest of bourgeois values.

Sartre himself lived to see the tradition of existentialism move beyond him. From the beginning it resisted anyone's attempt to monopolize it. Already in 1945 in his first statement on it, he said, "The word is now so loosely applied to so many things that it no longer means anything at all." Perhaps it was he who moved on. He is quoted in later life saying that Marxism is the only philosophy.

. . .
OR MAYBE WE ARE AT THE MERCY OF THE TITANIC FORCES OF HISTORY.

Albert Camus

(November 7, 1913 – January 4, 1960)

"There is but one truly serious philosophical question and that is suicide," wrote Albert Camus in his philosophical study *The Myth of Sisyphus*. *"Judging whether life is or is not worth living amounts to answering the fundamental question of philosophy. All the rest—whether or not the world has three dimensions, whether the mind has nine or twelve categories— comes afterwards. These are games; one must first answer. And if it is true, as Nietzsche claims, that a philosopher, to deserve our respect, must preach by example, you can appreciate the importance of that reply, for it will precede the definitive act. These are facts the heart can feel; yet they call for careful study before they become clear to the intellect."*

KEEP ASKIN'.

Camus' eloquent statements of existential problems are lucid and without frills. He was a clear thinker in the French tradition of Descartes. Though one of the foremost writers associated with existentialism, he did not consider himself an existentialist. Like most of the others, he rejected the label and preferred to be seen as an individual and a thinker, not a member of a group or ideology. In an interview in 1945, he said, "No, I am not an existentialist. Sartre and I are always surprised to see our names linked..."

He was born in Mondovi, Algeria, to a family of French settlers. His mother was of Spanish lineage. His father Lucien died only months after he was born in the World War I Battle of Marne. He grew up in impoverished circumstances in the Belcourt section of the city of Algiers. He was accepted into the University of Algiers, but he caught tuberculosis in 1930, which forced him to stop participating in soccer and cut his studies to part time. He took various jobs, as a tutor, a clerk at a car parts store and an attendant at the Meteorological Institute.

He married Simone Hie, a morphine addict, in 1934. The marriage was rocky, with affairs on both sides, and lasted only two years. He earned his BA in philosophy in 1935 and earned an equivalent of a Masters degree in 1936 with a thesis on Neo-Platonism.

The fascist takeover of Spain and French colonialist oppression in Algeria prompted him to join the Communist party in 1935. Never a doctrinaire Marxist-Leninist he was expelled from the party In 1937 for his involvement with the Algerian People's Party. He moved to France in 1940 and married again, to Francine Faure, a pianist and mathematician. They had two children, but Camus had difficulty with fidelity and his affairs, including one with the Spanish actress Maria Casares, put the marriage through trials.

I BEEN AROUND THE BLOCK- It's PHILO-SOPHICAL.

The Writer

"People can only think in images," he wrote in his journals in 1938. "If you want to be a philosopher, write novels." However, he reasoned, the task was more than just being able to write. "The problem is to acquire that knowledge of life (or rather to have lived) which goes beyond the mere ability to write. So that, in the last analysis, the great artist is first and foremost a man who has had a great experience of life." And so he would.

Though he could not have foreseen it then, Camus was to get more than his share of intense experience to form his character as a writer. Like the other French existentialists, Camus' philosophy was tempered by his experience during the Nazi invasion and occupation of France.

Living in Paris in 1940, he started writing for *Paris-Soire* magazine taking the stance of a pacifist. But after he experienced the Nazis' barbarism, particularly after he witnessed the shooting execution of Gabriel Peri, an anti-fascist journalist, he committed himself to the Resistance. In 1940 he became editor of *Combat*, an underground newspaper of the resistance network of the same name. It was through his work at *Combat* that he met Sartre, beginning what would be a stormy relationship.

He described his evolution from pacifist to confirmed militant against the Nazi occupation in a series of "Letters to a German Friend" published in *Combat* (later published in the book *Resistance, Rebellion and Death*). Written in 1943 and 1944, the letters condemned his German friend for giving up himself and his ideals of justice and truth to the Fatherland. Speaking for himself, he said that though the French's devotion to those ideals made it hard initially to resort to violence, it eventually led to greater strength.

The French were caught off guard by the Nazi onslaught, he wrote, because of "a detour that safeguarded justice and put truth on the side of those who questioned themselves. And, without a doubt, we paid very dearly for it. We paid for it with humiliations and silences, with bitter experiences, with prison sentences, with executions at dawn, with desertions and separations, with daily pangs of hunger, with emaciated children, and, above all, with humiliation of our human dignity... It took us all that time to find out if we had the right to kill men, if we were allowed to add to the frightful misery of the world. And because of that time lost and recaptured, our defeat accepted and surmounted, those scruples paid for with blood, we French had the right to think today that we entered this war with hands clean... For three years you have brought night to our towns and to our hearts. For three years we have been developing in the dark the thought which now emerges fully to face you."

Fascism would be defeated, Camus believed, because the human aspiration for freedom and justice is an ever-renewing force of nature.

"For you, Europe is a property, whereas we feel that we belong to it," Camus wrote. *"For all those landscapes, those flowers and those plowed fields, the oldest of lands, show you every spring that there are things you cannot choke in blood. That is the image on which I can close. It would not be enough for me to think that all the great states of the West and that thirty nations were on our side; I could not do it without the soil. And so I know that everything in Europe, both landscape and spirit, calmly negates you without feeling any rash hatred, but with the calm strength of victory... The battle we are waging is sure of victory because it is as obstinate as spring ... henceforth we have a superiority that will destroy you..."*

After the war *Combat* became a commercial paper and Camus left it.

Though he became a militant in opposition to the Nazis, Camus remained at heart a humanist, deeply concerned about the welfare of people, and was one of the few French writers who objected to the Americans dropping of the atomic bomb on Japan.

The Books

Camus wrote the bestselling novels *The Stranger* in 1942 and *The Plague* in 1947, and the philosophical studies *The Myth of Sisyphus* in 1942 and *The Rebel* in 1951.

In *The Stranger* he consciously borrowed the taut language of Ernest Hemingway to tell of a man who commits a pointless murder and is sentenced to die, which creates a platform upon which Camus can illustrate the absurdity of life. As his character contemplates his appeal, he assumes that it will not succeed. "That meant, of course, I was to die. Sooner than others, obviously. 'But,' I reminded myself, 'it's common knowledge that life isn't worth living anyhow,' And, on a wide view, I could see that it makes little difference whether one dies at the age of thirty or threescore and ten—since, in either case, other men and women will continue living, the world will go on as before. Also, whether I died now or forty years hence, this business of dying had to be got through, inevitably. Still, somehow this line of thought wasn't as consoling as it should have been, the idea of all those years of life in hand was a galling reminder!"

In *The Myth of Sisyphus* Camus considers what he calls the most fundamental question: Is life worth living? "It is legitimate and necessary to wonder whether life has a meaning; therefore it is legitimate to meet the problem of suicide face to face. The answer, underlying and appearing through the paradoxes which cover it is this: even if one does not believe in God, suicide is not legitimate." The book was written when most of Europe was under the heel of Nazi domination. But even so, Camus declared years later, the book "sums itself up as a lucid invitation to live and to create, in the very midst of the desert."

In *The Rebel* Camus applies the clarity of his intelligence to the act of rebellion. He portrays rebellion as an essential part of existence and says that in our time it has evolved from the rebellion of slave to master to a rebellion against the very conditions of life. In fact, the rise of civilization itself, he says, could be seen as an act of rebellion against the absurd circumstances of existence.

"Metaphysical rebellion is a claim, motivated by the concept of a complete unity, against the suffering of life and death and a protest against the human condition both for its incompleteness, thanks to death, and its wastefulness, thanks to evil. If a mass death sentence defines the human condition, then rebellion, in one sense, is its contemporary. At the same time that he rejects his mortality, the rebel refuses to recognize the power that compels him to life in this condition." Though he rebels against the almighty forces that place him in his circumstances, Camus says, the metaphysical rebel is not an atheist. "If the metaphysical rebel ranges himself against a power whose existence he simultaneously affirms, he only admits the existence of this power at the very instant that he calls it into question."

He points out that in the modern world, revolution always leads to further consolidation of power by the State. Modern man tore down the structures of authority of the church only to replace it with an even more powerful institution. "The strange and terrifying growth of the modern State can be considered as the logical conclusion of inordinate technical and philosophical ambitions, foreign to the true spirit of rebellion, but which nevertheless gave birth to the revolutionary spirit of our time. The prophetic dream of Marx and the over-inspired predictions of Hegel or of Nietzsche ended by conjuring up, after the city of God had been razed to the ground a rational or irrational State, which in both cases, however, was founded on terror."

The central theme in Camus' work is the absurd, rational man against an indifferent universe. In his view, life is rendered meaningless by the fact of death, and human beings cannot make rational sense of life. He called himself an atheist but had more in common with Martin Buber, who was religious, than with Sartre, who was an atheist. He said that he wouldn't mind being called religious in the sense of Buber's religiousness. But he did not accept Kierkegaard's idea of a leap of religious faith, which he called "philosophical suicide." He dismissed transcendence as pointless hope.

The Humanist

HEY, WE MIGHT BE ALONE, BUT YOU KNOW, WE'RE ALL IN THIS TOGETHER

In the 1950s he devoted himself to human rights working with UNESCO until he resigned in protest when the UN admitted Spain under the fascist regime of Franco. He protested Soviet oppression of the people of East Germany, Poland, and Hungary. He won the Nobel Prize for literature in 1957, the second youngest man, after Rudyard Kipling, to ever receive it.

He sympathized with Sartre's and Merleau-Ponty's attempts to create a New Left, but broke with them over their assertion that the end justifies the means and their support of Soviet Communism, which Camus found abhorrent because of its totalitarianism, just as he did the totalitarianism of the Nazis. Camus disagreed with Sartre's violence and his lack of humanism. Sartre disagreed with the absence of commitment in Camus' philosophy. Camus had been unable to make a commitment regarding

127

the Algerian War of Independence in 1954, saying that he felt for both sides. He said he was worried for his mother, who still lived in Algeria. Sartre once gave Camus a black eye. Sartre, a womanizer, may have been jealous of Camus' movie star looks. At the time of Camus' death, their quarrels remained unreconciled.

After the 1956 Hungarian revolt against Soviet domination was crushed by the Red Army, Camus wrote, "I am not one of those who think that there can be a compromise, even one made with resignation, even provisional, with a regime of terror which has as much right to call itself socialist as the executioners of the Inquisition had to call themselves Christians. And on this anniversary of liberty, I hope with all my heart that the silent resistance of the people of Hungary will endure, will grow stronger, and, reinforced by all the voices which we can raise on their behalf, will induce unanimous international opinion to boycott their oppressors."

Camus was killed in a car crash on January 4, 1960. He had an unused train ticket in his pocket, which probably meant he had planned to take the train, but changed his mind and took a ride with his publisher and close friend Michel Gallimard, the driver of the car.

In Sartre's obituary of Camus, he called him a "Cartesian of the Absurd." Camus' death seemed exemplary of his belief in an absurd, indifferent universe.

"I do not believe it..." Sartre said of Camus' death. "For all those who loved him, there was an unbearable absurdity in this death. But we shall have to learn to see this mutilated life-work as a whole life work... In the same measure that the humanism of Camus contained a humane attitude towards the death that was to take him by surprise, in the measure that his proud quest for human happiness implied and reclaimed the inhuman necessity of dying, we shall recognize in this work and in the life which is inseparable from it, the pure and victorious endeavor of a man to recover each instant of his existence from his future death."

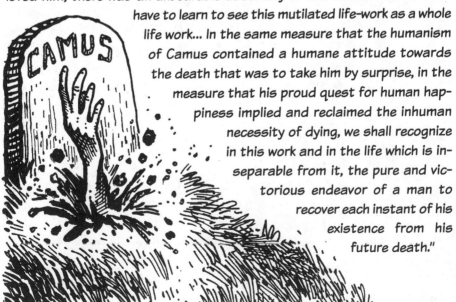

Simone de Beauvoir

(January 9, 1908 - April 14, 1986)

Simone de Beauvoir's life and work were closely intertwined with Sartre's, whom she met in 1929 at La Sorbonne, the University of Paris, after he saw her give a presentation on the German mathematician and philosopher Gottfried Wilhelm Leibniz. Throughout the rest of their lives Beauvoir and Sartre were intellectual compatriots, friends and lovers.

De Beauvoir is left out of most of the texts on existential philosophy, no doubt in part because she was a woman and in part because of her proximity to Sartre, whose dominating presence and prodigious output dominated the scene. But in the twenty-first century these facts make her that much more important as part of the movement and its principal feminine voice.

Who can say what her contribution to the development of Sartre's own ideas as a lifelong intellectual companion and partner? And vice versa. She was his most trusted critic and read his manuscripts before he sent them out. He returned the favor with her writings. But she also made her own individual contributions to the existential tradition, as well as making her mark as a major novelist and a feminist.

HE'S JUST SO IRRESISTABLE.

Bourgeois Baby

She was born in Paris into a middle class family, elder of two daughters of a lawyer, who was also an actor and an impulsive businessman. She was raised as a Catholic in the traditional bourgeois tradition, but rebelled against the social values of her class when she was an adolescent.

She was educated in Catholic schools, majoring in mathematics, then languages, and then studied philosophy at the Sorbonne, where she picked up the nickname "Castor," which means "beaver" in French and referred to the similarity of the name Beauvoir to "beaver" in English. She was the youngest person to pass the civil service test for philosophy, which was required for some teaching jobs in the public school system. She received it the same year as Sartre, who had taken the test the previous year and failed it.

She taught philosophy in a number of schools in Paris, Marseille and Rouen. She was a professor at the Sorbonne from 1941-43, then dismissed by the Nazi authorities.

With Sartre and Merleau-Ponty, she was one of the founders of Modern Times. Not just a follower of Sartre, she cut her own path and made her own place in philosophy. Her 1947 book *The Ethics of Ambiguity* provides an existential ethics, which is something Sartre himself, in all his voluminous writings, did not do.

The Second Existentialist

Her novels dealt with existentialist themes in a literary dramatic form, using action to illustrate the themes, an appropriate form for explaining a philosophy in which action defines and creates reality. Her writing portrayed her belief that a writer should be committed to political action to confront issues of the times.

She was acclaimed for her novels *L'Invitée* (*She Came to Stay*) and *Les Mandarins* (*The Mandarins*), which were autobiographical stories in which a fictionalized Sartre appears as a character. She wrote monographs on philosophy, politics and social issues, essays and biographies.

She chronicled her life in a four-volume autobiography, *Memoirs of a Dutiful Daughter*.

In *L'Invitée*, Beauvoir wrote about an affair Sartre had with Olga Kosakievics. In the book she describes having a ménage a trois with the two of them. In the turmoil that ensued in the love triangle, Pierre, the Sartre character, tells Francoise (Beauvoir), "You and I are simply one. That is the truth, you know. Neither of us can be described without the other."

Her 1945 book *Le Sang des autres* (*The Blood of Others*) was written before the end of the war and depicts a relationship between a wealthy young man who breaks with his family to join the Communist party, and a young individualist woman who does not share his commitment. It was filmed in 1982, starring Jodie Foster as the female lead.

In 1947 she published *The Ethics of Ambiguity*, in which she created a basic for ethics for existentialists. She draws on Sartre's work, but adds the component of ethics. She argued that the nonexistence of God does not mean that there is no need for ethics. Without God, in fact, there is even more need for ethics because human beings are completely responsible for themselves.

"If man is free to define for himself the conditions of a life which is valid in his own eyes, can he not choose whatever he likes and act however he likes? Dostoyevsky asserted, "If God does not exist, everything is permitted." Today's believers use this formula for their own advantage. To re-establish man at the heart of his destiny is, they claim, to repudiate all ethics. However, far from God's absence authorizing all license, the contrary is the case, because man is abandoned on the earth, because his acts are definitive, absolute engagements. He bears the responsibility for a world which is not the work of a strange power, but of himself, where his defeats are inscribed, and his victories as well. A God can pardon, efface, and compensate. But if God does not exist, man's faults are inexpiable. If it is claimed that, whatever the case may be, this earthly stake has no importance, this is precisely because one invokes that inhuman objectivity which we declined at the start. One can not start by saying that our earthly destiny has or has not importance, for it depends upon us to give it importance. It is up to man to make it important to be a man, and he alone can feel his success or failure."

Her 1949 book *The Second Sex*, an analysis of the historic oppression of women, is one of the primary feminist texts, as well as a presentation of existential feminism. She wrote that "one is not born, but rather becomes, a woman," and that "in all known societies, woman has always been looked upon as the other."

In her 1954 book *Les Mandarins*, Beauvoir appears again in a love triangle with Sartre. This time the third party was based on the American novelist Nelson Algren, whom she met in 1947 in the U.S. when she was on a lecture tour. He wanted to marry her, but she remained loyal to Sartre, whom she told Algren, "was a warm lively man everywhere, but not in bed." In his reviews of the American translations of Beauvoir's books, he expressed his outrage at the sexual frankness of her writings about their relationship in *Les Mandarins* and in general in her autobiography. In the book, Beauvoir urges leftist intellectuals to drop their Mandarin, or elitist tendencies, and join the political struggles of the real world. *Les Mandarins* won the prestigious Prix Goncourt award.

She traveled widely, often with Sartre, to Switzerland, Italy, Portugal, Tunisia, the U.S. and China. With Sartre she met Soviet Premier Nikita Khruschev and Cuban President Fidel Castro, but the experience was not her cup of tea. In 1967 she participated with Sartre and English philosopher Bertrand Russell in a Tribunal of War Crimes in Vietnam.

In 1981, a year after Sartre died, she published *La Cérémonie Des Adieux (A Farewell to Sartre)*, a tortured account of Sartre's last years. It is the only one of her major published works that he did not read before it was published.

In 1990, she published some of Sartre's letters. Names were changed to protect those mentioned, and many of them had to be edited after disputes with Arlette Elkaim, a Jewish Algerian, whom Sartre had adopted and who became the heir to his literary works.

In her later years, her love of alcohol slowed her down. She had always been a big drinker and also, like Sartre, took drugs, mostly amphetamines. She died of pneumonia in 1986 and is buried next to Sartre in Paris.

Gabriel Marcel

December 7, 1889 Paris – October 8, 1973

Though Gabriel Marcel has been credited with coining the term "existentialism" as a way to refer to the works of Jean Paul Sartre and Simone de Beauvoir, he did not like being categorized that way himself. He didn't like being grouped with Jean Paul Sartre and preferred to call himself "neo-Socratic." Marcel was one of those at the center of the Postwar French existentialist culture, though he was in many ways opposed to Sartre. His sources were not the German ones of Sartre, but the American idealist Josiah Royce and the French intuitionist or vitalist Henri Bergson. He developed an existential philosophy before he was familiar with the writings of Kierkegaard, Heidegger and Jaspers. Bergson believed that abstract thinking was insufficient to grasp the richness of experience. He also referred to the irreducible reality of time and said that the depth of the psychic life evaded quantitative methods of measurement.

JUST BECAUSE I CALL 'EM DOESN'T MAKE ME ONE OF 'EM.

In Marcel's *Metaphysical Journal*, he describes the development of his thought, which derives more from personal experience than from reading philosophy. He found abstract philosophy to be incomplete in dealing with his real experiences.

He was born in Paris in 1889, the son of a French diplomat. He lost his mother with he was four years old and then developed a rich fantasy life as he learned to communicate with the characters of his imagination. He wrote his first two plays at the age of eight. He is an example of how the action of the theater is in some ways a more suitable place to demonstrate the ideas of existentialism than essays. "In the drama and by means of the drama metaphysical thought seizes itself and determines itself in the concrete," he wrote.

Beyond Atheism

His father was an atheist, and he began as an atheist. But he found an emptiness in himself and his environment that oppressed him. His philosophic inquiry brought him to the subject of religious faith. Though an unbeliever, he became interested an interest in the faith of others and began to analyze philosophically the act of faith.

During World War I he served in the Red Cross and was shaken by the daily inquiries of the next of kin of soldiers missing in action. It pushed him from idealism to a more concrete, existential humanism. He kept a notebook from 1914 in which he traced the evolution of his thinking as it gravitated more toward the thought of Kierkegaard. His journals were published in 1927 as *Metaphysical Journal*. He ultimately left more than fifty journals that are archived, and many of which were published.

In the Societe francaise de Philosophie, during a discussion of atheism, he defended the validity of religious faith and a few month later received a letter from the French Catholic writer Francois Mauriac asking, "Why are you not one of us?" In 1929 he became a Catholic.

The Dramatist

He wrote plays as a schoolboy and in the early 1920s he began having his plays performed. He was also a musician who enjoyed improvisations on the piano and after World War II he began setting down compositions, including musical interpretations of the poems of Baudelaire and Rilke.

Starting with being-in-the-world, Marcel asks, "How can I accept my human situation and make it the starting point of becoming a human person?" The answer cannot be given in an abstract theory, he says, it can only be found in contact with concrete reality, in engagement, and ultimately in an act of faith. Engagement is three-fold: confronting my present, accepting my past and projecting my future. By affirming myself in my personality, I oppose the collective mass man. As the featureless "das Man," I cannot realize myself, cannot engage.

Philosophic rationalism misses its goal because it regards as true only that wich can be either rationally or scientifically verified. It defines truth as an agreement of minds reached by the individual relinquishing his own thought in favor of "thought in general." But the ultimate truth can never be a truth that comes about in this way. It is personal and incommunicable. In the state of Perfect Faith, one rises above objectivity and experiences God in the pure actuality of an Absolute Presence.

Where for Sartre, man is "thrown" into a hostile world and abandoned to his own devices, for Marcel man is not left to realize his destiny in total solitude. His life is guided by values which are not of his own making but are themselves "incarnate" in "being." For Sartre, values exist only as the choice of a man, for Marcel, the values are the basis of choice. The values can, however, be negated in favor of the absurd.

The impersonal thinking of the mass, of "das Man," based on the "thinking substance" of Descartes or the "transcendental ego" of Kant, is not real. A world view based on "thought in general" will collapse in self-destruction and despair. Philosophical and metaphysical knowledge is opposed to "das Man." "The immortal glory of a Kierkegaard or a Nietzsche," he writes, "consists ... in having demonstrated, not so much by rational arguments as by their lives, that a philosopher worthy of the name is not, cannot be, and must not be a man of the public, of meetings and conventions; that he debases himself to the extent that he allows himself to be deprived of that solitude which is his proper vocation."

Maurice Merleau-Ponty

(March 14, 1908 – May 4, 1961)

Only three years his junior, Maurice Merleau-Ponty was closely connected in time and place with Sartre. He studied at the École Normale Supérieure with Sartre, and when Sartre was released from being a prisoner of war in 1941, he formed an "intellectual resistance" group with Merleau-Ponty. With Sartre and Simone de Beauvoir, Merleau-Ponty was a cofounder in 1945 of *Les Temps Moderne*, a monthly review that commented on the postwar world.

> A MIND AIN'T WORTH MUCH WITHOUT A BODY.

He was considered one of the core group of French existentialists that included Sartre and de Beauvoir, but did not share their intensity on some of the principles they are known for, such as radical freedom, being towards death, anguished responsibility and conflicting relations with others. Instead he focused on the analysis of perception and consciousness. His work is held in high regard today for its relevance to medical ethics, cognitive science, psychology, sociology and even ecology. Like Sartre and Heidegger, Merleau-Ponty studied Husserl's phenomenology and used it as a starting point to jump off in an existential direction. His *Structure of Behavior* offers an alternative to the Cartesian body/mind separation. The body, he asserted, had long been underestimated in philosophy and treated as a machine that is directed by a transcendent mind. But the body has a great deal to do with how we perceive and experience reality.

> OR A SHADOW, EITHER.

In *The Phenomenology of Perception*, published in 1952, he critiqued Husserl's phenomenology, tracing where he thought it went astray and coming up with his own formulation. He put forth the phenomenological objection to positivism: that science can tell us nothing about the human subjectivity, the experience of being human.

In his essay "What is Phenomenology?" he wrote, "Everything that I know, even through science, I know on the basis of a view which is my own, or an experience of the world without which the symbols of science would be meaningless."

He explained Husserl's motto, "To the things themselves," in this way: "To turn back to the things themselves is to return to that world prior to knowledge of which knowledge speaks, and with regard to which every scientific determination is abstractive, dependent and a sign; it is like the relationship of geography to the countryside where we first learned what forest, a prairie or a river was."

He rejected the Cartesian idea that life is all about thinking, and said that it is about acting, experiencing. Our perception of the real world is our fundamental access to truth. The world of science cannot be given a greater reality than the world of our perceptions, because it too is based on our perceptions. He came up with the body/mind subject as an alternative to Descartes' *cogito*, man as a thinking organism. It meant that one perceives the world existentially as opposed to the Cartesian sense of the world being just an extension of one's own mind. Consciousness, the world and the human body are all intricately interwoven and engaged with one another.

ALL THINKING AND NO ACTION WOULD MAKE MERLEAU-PONTY A DULL BOY, INDEED.

Though we can perceive things only in part, from a particular perspective in a unique place and time, this doesn't diminish the reality of what we see. There is no other way to perceive reality than from a relative, unique perspective. That which we perceive is connected to its background, its environment, and to the nexus of meaningful relationships with the world. So through our being-in-the-world, we are able to project other perspectives of the object of our perception.

Both empiricism and intellectualism, or rationalism, are flawed positions, he said. "In the first case consciousness is too poor, in the second too rich for any phenomenon to appeal compellingly to it. Empiricism cannot see that we need to know what we are looking for, otherwise we would not be looking for it, and intellectualism fails to see that we need to be ignorant of what we are looking for, or equally again we should not be searching"

He achieved a high ranking in the academic world. After the publication of *Phenomenology of Perception*, he was elected to the chair of philosophy at the College de France. Merleau-Ponty was involved in the political left before Sartre. His book *Humanism and Terror*, had a profound effect on Sartre. It coincided with his and Sartre's disillusionment with the communist party. Merleau-Ponty maintained an individualistic stance in relation to politics, which drove him away from the left and precipitated his eventual estrangement from Sartre.

He died suddenly of a stroke in 1961 at the age of 53.

Jose Ortega y Gasset

(May 9, 1883 - October 18, 1955)

"Once again, man has lost himself. For this is nothing new, nothing accidental. Man has been lost many times throughout the course of his history. Indeed, it is of the essence of man, in contradistinction to all other beings, that he can lose himself, lose himself in the jungle of his existence, within himself, and thanks to this sensation of being lost can react by setting energetically to work to find himself again. His ability to feel lost and his discomfort at feeling lost are his tragic destiny and his illustrious privilege."

—Ortega & Gasset,
from "The Personal Life" in Man and People.

Jose Ortega y Gasset was a Spanish thinker who was profoundly influenced by German philosophy. He is best known for his 1930 book *Revolt of the Masses*, in which he describes the effects of bureaucracy, specialization, standardization, mass production and cultural mediocrity on the European spirit. He wrote about many of the same themes as Heidegger—in most cases earlier and in a more down-to-earth vocabulary.

Existential themes of Ortega y Gasset include the idea of life as uneasiness, preoccupation and insecurity, and of culture as the preoccupation with security; of life as the confrontation of the I and its
environment; the structure of life as futurition, or leaning into the future;
the idea of truth as "disclosure, unwrapping, uncovering,"; philosophy as
consubstantial (of the same essential material) with human life because
life has to go out into the "world," philosophy is not the sum of things
but the horizon of totality above things and distinct from them; the effort to transmute pure reason to vital reason.

He was born to a Madrid newspaper family. His mother's family owned
the Madrid newspaper and his father was a journalist and director of the
paper. He was first educated by Jesuits, then studied at The University
of Deusto in Bilbao and Complutense University in Madrid, earning a doctorate in philosophy. Then he went to Germany to study at Leipzig,
Nuremberg, Cologne, Berlin, and Marburg, where he was influenced by
Neo-Kantianism. Then returned to Madrid to teach.

He was politically engaged and helped to found a number of publications. He resigned his post as professor in protest against the military dictator Primo de Rivera, who took power in 1923. He didn't think the monarchy could still win the belief of the people, so advocated the formation of a liberal democratic republic. After the fall of Rivera in 1930, and the abdication of King Alfonso XIII, he sat in the constituent assembly of the Second Republic in 1931-32, was deputy for the province of Leon and Civil Governor of Madrid. He spent one year as an elected representative to the parliament, then became disillusioned and withdrew from politics.

He believed philosophy has a duty to attack beliefs and come up with new ideas in order to explain life and reality. To do this, he agreed with Husserl, that one must cast aside prejudices and beliefs and try to see directly what is happening. Descartes' "I think therefore I am" was insufficient to explain life, he said, and instead put forth the idea that "I am myself and my circumstances," he said. Though I cannot control the circumstances in which I find myself, I do have freedom to act. Therefore life plays out as a drama in the tension between necessity, or fate, and freedom. Freedom, he said, "is being free inside of a given fate. Fate gives us an inexorable repertory of determinate possibilities, that is, it gives us different destinies. We accept fate and within it we choose one destiny." He advocated being active, making choices and creating a "project of life" in order to rise beyond the conventional life enmired in customs and established systems.

EXCUSE ME, I'LL FLY.

False Dawns

In *Revolt of the Masses*, he refers to "the masses" in his own way, not in the sense of the working class, but similarly to how other existential writers have referred to the herd, "the they," etc. "The mass is the average man," he wrote. "In this way what was mere quantity – the multitude – is converted into a qualitative determination: it becomes the common social quality, man as undifferentiated from other men, but as repeating in himself a generic man."

He saw liberal democracy as "the loftiest endeavor towards the common life," and declared the "new" revolutions of Bolshevism and Fascism as "retrogression" that were leading towards "barbarism" and "the primitivism of a man who has no past, or who has forgotten it."

"Both Bolshevism and Fascism are two false dawns," he wrote. "They do not bring the morning of a new day, but of some archaic day, spent over and over again." In diametric opposition to the claims of Hegel, Ortega called the State, "The Greatest Danger."

Ortega said that only your own life is really real to you. It is your "radical reality" because it is at the root of your understanding of everything else and everyone else. He pointed out that the word *exist* had lost its earlier meaning when it carried connotations of struggle and confrontation, and had grown to mean something passive, something that just is, like a stone. Like other existential thinkers, Ortega distinguished between the existence of a rock or an inanimate object and that kind of existence that is only possible for a human. The part of you that is just you is the only part that *exists* in this sense. "...life is not something that we have bestowed on ourselves; rather we find it precisely when we find ourselves. Suddenly and without knowing how or why, without any previous forewarning of it, man sees and finds that he is obliged to have his being in an unpremeditated, unforeseen gambit, in a conjunction of completely definite circumstances." We cannot choose the world we live in, but within that world we have choices. "To live or to be alive or, what is the same thing, to be a man, does not admit of any preparations or preliminary experiments. Life is fired at us point blank..."

"...there is no escape: we have something to do or have to be doing something *always;* for this life that is given us is not given us ready-made, but instead every one of us has to make it for himself, each his own. This life that is given us is given us empty, and man has to keep filling it for himself, occupying it. Such is our occupation." Escape is possible from even the most extreme circumstances, if one is "between the sword and the wall" one may choose one or the other, a hero's death or a coward's death. What is not escapable is having to do something, having to make choices, having to make your life into something."

Radical Solitude

Man lives in "radical solitude" because only he can really feel his own pain, but his radical solitude does not mean he is the only one in the world. On the contrary, man must live with the whole universe. But in terms of the decisions that will create the form of your life, you are alone. No one can be in your place and make those decisions for you.

His essay "In Search of Goethe from Within" is a discussion of the problem of living an authentic life in harmony with one's true destiny, one's "inner I."

"*Man recognizes his I, his unique vocation, only through the liking or aversion aroused in him by each separate situation. Unhappiness, like the needle of a registering apparatus, tells him when his actual life realizes his vital program, his entelechy and when it departs from it... Only his sufferings and his satisfactions instruct him concerning himself. ...*

Life consists in giving up the state of availability. Mere availability is the characteristic of youth faced with maturity. The youth, because he is not yet anything determinate and irrevocable, is everything potentially. Herein lies his charm and his insolence. Feeling that he is everything potentially, he supposes that he is everything actually... The growing insecurity of his existence proceeds to eliminate possibilities, matures him... Serious economic difficulties begin, the struggle with the rest of mankind begins... But if at this period, instead of coming against the world's resistance for the first time, we find it giving way before us, roused to no waves by our passage, fulfilling our desires with magic docility, our I will fall voluptuously asleep; instead of being revealed to itself, it remains vague. Nothing so saps the profound resources of a life as finding life too easy."

Existential Theater
Theatre of the Absurd

In the 1950s the Theatre of the Absurd emerged, drawing on the works of Sartre and Camus, including Camus' adaptation of Dostoyevsky's *The Possessed*, for stage in 1959. It also had precedents in the works of Franz Kafka and Luigi Pirandello.

Sartre's *No Exit* was perhaps the archetypal piece of Existential Theater. The Theatre of the Absurd drew on the ideas of Sartre and Camus that mankind must face an absurd universe, that a rational explanation of the universe is not within the powers of man, so one must live with this realization, and still try to find meaning in life.

JUST WAIT WE'LL FIND IT.

Theater of the Absurd posed existential problems in the form of plays, which provide a way to pose problems in action, in time, which are possibilities of theater that make it one of the most suitable forms through which to explore existential themes.

HOW THE HELL DO WE GET OUTTA HERE?

The name Theater of the Absurd was coined by Martin Esslin to describe the plays of Eugene Ionesco, Jean Genet, Arthur Adamov, Samuel Beckett, Harold Pinter and other playwrights. Esslin wrote that, the sense of metaphysical anguish at the absurdity of the human condition is Theatre of the Absurd's underlying theme.

He wrote that although Sartre and Camus dealt with a new way of seeing the world, they wrote in forms that were traditional, rationalistic forms of the eighteenth century, and the Theatre of the Absurd had thrown out the need for consistently drawn characters and logical plot.

He saw Theatre of the Absurd as part of a larger anti-literary movement that had a kinship to Abstract Expressionist painting, in which literal themes are rejected in favor of pure intuitive and emotional expressions.

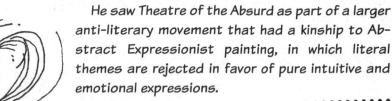

"LIVE FAST, DIE YOUNG, AND LEAVE A BEAUTIFUL CORPSE". WHAT COULD BE MORE EXISTENTIAL THAN THAT?

Existential Film

Existential theater and existential philosophy in general also found its expression in film.

In the early 1950s, James Dean became known as an existential archetype in his roles in *East of Eden* and *Rebel Without a Cause*. Elia Kazan, director of discovered Dean playing the role of an Arab boy in a Broadway adaptation of Andre Gide's *The Immoralist*, a story about a character modeled on Nietzsche.

Dean became a new kind of existential character in cinema. He played in some twenty TV shows in New York before going to Hollywood for his three big films. He threw himself so far into his roles that his personal life became affected, began to come unraveled. He had torrid love affairs, raced cars, played bongos. And at the end of his filming of his third film *Giant* he was killed on the highway as he drove his Porsche toward where he was going to participate in an auto race. A week before he had filmed a highway safety commercial. He became the model for a generation of alienated youth. He was Elvis Presley's model for his personal style. A cult grew around him and many of the youth of the next generation, including Bob Dylan and Jim Morrison, identified with him and were compared with him.

ME, I'M MISTER EXISTENTIAL.

Jean-Luc Godard's *Breathless*, was seen as an archetypal existential film with Jean-Paul Belmondo portraying a typically existential hero, also derivative of Dean, but placing the existential anti-hero back in a French setting, where existentialism began, in a sense. In the twenty-first century, existential themes have so deeply permeated the culture that one can practically pick a film at random and find it rests on them. Picking a film almost at random – one that was on cable TV the day this book was written— *The Island*, with Ewan McGregor, Scarlett Johannsson and Djimon Hounsou, for example. Clones grown in an organ farm, supposedly a completely controlled environment so that they remain nothing more than sources for organs, and yet the attempt by the scientist man-gods to control life fails. The clones become self aware, the system cannot hold back the force of life. One sees the light, discovers the fraud, takes a leap against nearly hopeless odds and manages to escape, to topple the control structures. He says, "There's only one thing you can count on, that people will do anything to survive."

The same themes are present in *The Matrix*, *Blade Runner*, *Frankenstein* and – you name it – hundreds of other films.

Existential Music

The smooth, mannered pop music of Sinatra's age in the '40s and early '50s gave way to the raw sensuality of blues-influenced rock and roll in Elvis Presley, which took popular music from an ivory tower view of the world down into the street and made the music more existential than the polite forms that preceded it. Then with the advent of the Beatles and Bob Dylan in the 1960s, rock and roll took on an expanded literary component. And that literature had a decidedly existential bent.

The characteristic spirit of the '60s began with the assassination of John F. Kennedy, the brutal struggles between segregation and the civil rights movement and the war in Vietnam. Those events mark the loss of American innocence and co-incide with the emergence of the new, more literary rock and roll. Some of the most memorable, striking works were statements of existential themes, one of the best of which was Bob Dylan's "It's Alright Ma, I'm Only Bleeding."

> HOW MANY EXISTENTIAL SONGS CAN A MAN WRITE DOWN . . .

Darkness at the break of noon,
Shadows even the silver spoon
The handmade blade, the child's balloon,
Eclipses both the sun and moon,
To understand you know to soon,
There is no sense in trying

Pointed threats, they bluff with scorn
Suicide remarks are torn
From the fool's gold mouthpiece
The hollow horn plays wasted words
Proves to warn
That he not busy being born
Is busy dying.

The song is a stark portrait of American life from an existential point of view. Dylan describes eloquently the inauthentic life of the mass man living what Thoreau called "lives of quiet desperation."

For those who must obey authority
That they do not respect in any degree
Who despise their jobs, their destinies
Speak jealously of them that are free
Cultivate their flowers to be
Nothing more than something
They invest in.

In part inspired by Dylan, the Beatles also dug more deeply into their literary heritage and produced some memorable existential statements of their own, as in the John Lennon lyrics in the song "A Day in the Life."

I read the news today oh boy
About a lucky man who made the grade
And though the news was rather sad,
Well I just had to laugh.
I saw the photograph,
He blew his mind out in a car,
He didn't notice that the
*   lights had changed,*
A crowd of people stood
*   and stared,*
They'd seen his face before,
Nobody was really sure
If he was from the
*   House of Lords.*

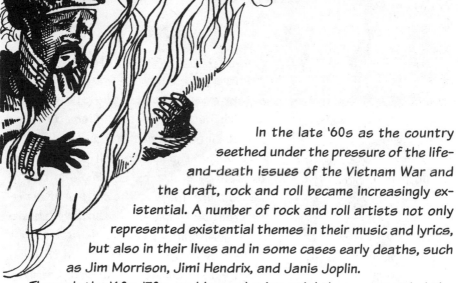

In the late '60s as the country seethed under the pressure of the life-and-death issues of the Vietnam War and the draft, rock and roll became increasingly existential. A number of rock and roll artists not only represented existential themes in their music and lyrics, but also in their lives and in some cases early deaths, such as Jim Morrison, Jimi Hendrix, and Janis Joplin.

Through the '60s, '70s, and beyond existential themes pervaded the literature of rock and roll. It continued into the '70s. A classic example of the American experience seen through existential eyes is Bruce Springsteen's "Born to Run."

In the day we sweat it out in the streets of a runaway American dream
At night we ride through mansions of glory in suicide machines
Sprung from cages out on Highway 9,
Chrome wheeled, fuel-injected and steppin' out over the line
Baby this town rips the bones from your back
It's a death trap, it's a suicide rap
We gotta get out while were young
　　'Cause tramps like us, baby we were born to run.

As with film, literature and other forms of creative expression, by the late twentieth century and beyond, existential themes are pervasive in music.

Existential Art

Though there was no notable group of painters and sculptors who called themselves existentialists, the spirit, mood and themes of existentialism did profoundly influence painting and sculpture.

Existential themes like self-creation, the existential leap, the uniqueness of the individual life are part the culture of artistic creation itself, so existentialism has a built-in kinship with all forms of art.

Surrealism, with its dedication to freedom, self-creation, the absurd, the irrational and its fearlessness in taking on the most intense subjects had an intrinsic affinity with the existentialists. Though existentialists urge unrelenting realism, and the surrealists celebrated flights of the imagination, the apparent contradiction dissolves past the surface in the fact that the word "surrealism" was derived from the concept of "super realism." In the Manifesto of Surrealism, Andre Breton wrote like an existentialist: "So strong is the belief in life, in what is most fragile in life – *real life*, I mean – that in the end this belief is lost." Breton describes surrealism as a reaction against positivism.

Some artists, including Franz Kafka, are called both existentialists and surrealists. The absurd and the surreal are closely linked.

Simone de Beauvoir said in 1965 that existentialism had influenced artists "to accept their transitory condition without renouncing a certain absolute, to face horror and absurdity while still retaining their human dignity." Existentialism reflected the mood of the Western world in mid century, and painters and sculptors were influenced by same forces as well as by the cultural force of the existentialist thinkers. Many of them more or less shared the existentialist view of life as a subjective, individual experience in an absurd world but with some hope of redemption by the power to make oneself through one's actions.

Jean Fautrier hid out in a mental asylum on the outskirts of Paris with other prisoners of the Nazis and could hear the Nazis torturing and executing prisoners. His work incorporates such horrors into his visual images and symbols. Alberto Giacometti depicted frail figures alienated and lost in wide spaces. Francis Bacon showed vivid images of violence, horror and claustrophobia.

Expressionists portrayed an angular, angst-ridden world that had much in common with the world of the existentialists.

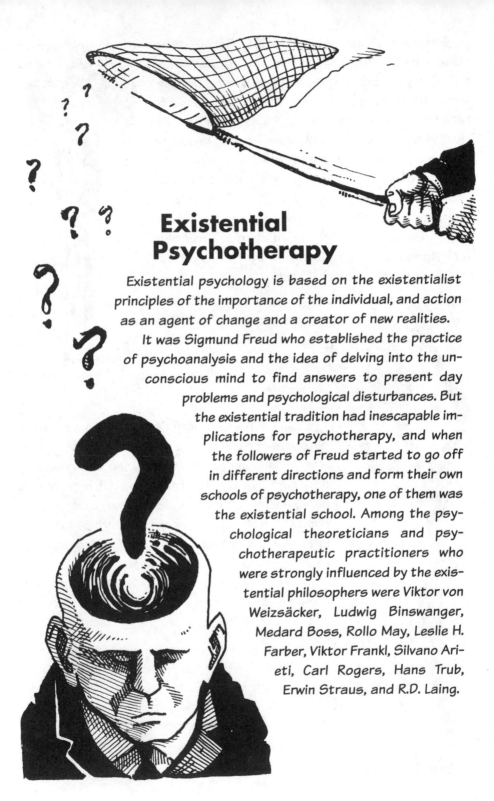

Existential Psychotherapy

Existential psychology is based on the existentialist principles of the importance of the individual, and action as an agent of change and a creator of new realities.

It was Sigmund Freud who established the practice of psychoanalysis and the idea of delving into the unconscious mind to find answers to present day problems and psychological disturbances. But the existential tradition had inescapable implications for psychotherapy, and when the followers of Freud started to go off in different directions and form their own schools of psychotherapy, one of them was the existential school. Among the psychological theoreticians and psychotherapeutic practitioners who were strongly influenced by the existential philosophers were Viktor von Weizsäcker, Ludwig Binswanger, Medard Boss, Rollo May, Leslie H. Farber, Viktor Frankl, Silvano Arieti, Carl Rogers, Hans Trub, Erwin Straus, and R.D. Laing.

Those who were influenced by existential philosophy drew their insights from the tradition going back to Kierkegaard's notions of anxiety and dread. "Dread is the dizziness of freedom which occurs when the spirit would posit the synthesis, and freedom then gazes down into its own possibility, grasping at finiteness to sustain itself. In this dizziness freedom succumbs. Further than this psychology cannot go and will not. That very instant everything is changed and when freedom rises again it sees that it is guilty. Between these two instants lies the leap, which no science has explained or can explain... Dread is a womanish debility in which freedom swoons. In dread there is the egoistic infinity of possibility, which does not tempt like a definite choice, but alarms and fascinates with its sweet anxiety."

Jaspers was a clinical psychologist before he was an existential philosopher, and the book he considers the first work of modern existentialism was titled *The Psychology of World Views*. But once again, Sartre set himself to the task of being the authoritative voice of existential psychotherapy in a section of his book *Being & Nothingness* titled "Existential Psychoanalysis." The essay was packaged with another section of *Being & Nothingness* called "Bad Faith and Falsehood" in a volume called "Existential Psychoanalysis" with a forward by Rollo May, one of the best-known of those known as existential psychologists.

According to May, the title of the book may lead one to think Sartre was going to offer an alternative style of psychoanalysis, but, he says, "This he neither does nor seeks to do; indeed, he rightly acknowledges that a genuine existential psychoanalysis cannot yet be formulated or written." Instead Sartre writes a critique of Freud's model of psychoanalysis. He objects to Freud's determinism, the idea that one's problems are caused by forces of which one is unconscious ran against the grain of his strong belief in personal responsibility. Sartre made some suggestions as to how an existential psychoanalysis might be developed.

He objected to dividing the human being into separate parts, the ego and the id and putting them against each other. It creates a way of justifying behavior by attributing it to the other, in this case a part of ourselves. Existential psychoanalysis would be based on the idea that "man is a totality and not a collection."

Sartre objected to the idea of normality, to the idea that one must try to adjust oneself to a "norm" or to fit into any social role. Man is not an object to be forced into any "role demanded by modern society – to be only a waiter or a conductor or a mother, only to be an employer or a worker," he wrote.

Jaspers objected to the turning of psychoanalysis into a faith, using formulas to define people and formulaic methods of "curing" them. The practice of psychotherapy as a means of one person helping another he considered a noble cause, but did not approve of making "a matter of mechanical technique what must always remain a matter of personal communication between individuals."

He disliked the idea that one could profess understanding of something merely by attributing it to a cause. "The understanding of the meaning of something that takes place in mutual communication: causality is foreign to this process and means recognizing something as different and distant."

The branch of psychology that is most at variance with existentialism is probably Behaviorism, a school of thought founded by B.F. Skinner in which human beings are treated as mechanical systems merely in terms of their behavior without any concern for the inner processes that produced the behavior. Behaviorism works to condition people in terms of basic operant conditioning: provide something they like, a positive experience, to reinforce positive behavior and punish undesirable behavior. Drawn to its logical conclusion, however, there would be no one to create and operate such a system. If one directs the logic of behaviorism to its creators themselves, as human beings and not gods, then the whole thing falls apart, as Carl Rogers, an existential psychologist, pointed out to Skinner himself in response to a paper presented by Skinner.

"From what I understood Dr. Skinner to say, it is his understanding that though he might have thought he chose to come to this meeting, might have thought he had a purpose in giving his speech, such thoughts are really illusory. He actually made certain marks on paper and emitted certain sounds here simply because of his genetic make-up and his past environment has operantly conditioned his behavior in such a way that it was rewarding to make these sounds, and that he as a person doesn't enter into this."

British psychologist R.D. Laing questioned the whole paradigm of normal/abnormal.

"The condition of alienation, of being asleep, of being unconscious, of being out of one's mind, is the condition of the normal man. Society highly values its normal man. It educates its children to lose themselves and become absurd, and thus to be normal. Normal men have killed perhaps 100,000,000 of their fellow men in the last fifty years."

Existential America

As Jaspers pointed out, and Paul Tillich later affirmed, existentialism emerged as if it were the species' response to its unique historical circumstances, first dawning in a few visionary individuals, spreading through the culture and eventually becoming the dominant mode of experiencing life in the twentieth century.

Although America stood somewhat separate from Europe during the emergence of existentialism, American culture has much affinity with existentialism and it has found a congenial home in America.

As a young, colonial offshoot of European culture, American culture has a youthful optimism and naiveté from the standpoint of the European. Unlike Europe, which was ravaged by the horrors of war in the first half of the twentieth century, America was relatively untouched by the world wars, at least on its own soil. But the existential view of life grew up indigenously in America as surely as it did in Europe, though with an American twist.

The U.S. had seen its own bloodbath in its Civil War of the nineteenth century, which reached historically new heights in savagery, and a new stage of modern warfare when the formal restraints of earlier wars marched head-on into total war and swords and muskets gave way to the more modern, more efficient technologically enabled methods of killing.

The American experience always carried within it an affinity to the existential spirit. As America was born and grew up at roughly the same time as existentialism, there are unavoidable parallels in their development.

In *Moby Dick*, Herman Melville wrote, "Though in many of its aspects this visible world seems formed in love, the invisible spheres were formed in fright.... As this appalling ocean surrounds the verdant land, so in the soul of man there lies one insular Tahiti, full of peace and joy, but encompassed by all the horrors of the half known life. God keep thee. Push not off from that isle, thou canst never return."

Nietzsche praised the American transcendentalist Ralph Waldo Emerson in his letters and essays, was profoundly moved by Emerson and was re-reading Emerson's "Self Reliance" when he first started putting together his ideas for *Thus Spake Zarathustra*. Emerson's ideas on the importance of the individual, on fate, history and nature were all powerful influences on Nietzsche.

Henry Miller, an American expatriate in Paris in the 1930s, wrote with fiery eloquence of the existential themes in his book *Tropic of Cancer*.

"*For weeks and months, for years, in fact, all my life I had been looking forward to something happening, some extrinsic event that would alter my life, and now suddenly, inspired by the absolute hopelessness of everything, I felt relieved, felt as though a great burden had been lifted from my shoulders...I decided to let myself drift with the tide, to make not the least resistance to fate, no matter in what form it presented itself. Nothing that had happened to me thus far had been sufficient to destroy me; nothing had been destroyed except my illusions. I myself was intact. The world was intact. Tomorrow there might be a revolution, a plague, an earthquake; tomorrow there might not be left a single soul to whom one could turn for sympathy, for aid, for faith. It seemed to me that the great calamity had already manifested itself, that I could be no more truly alone than at this very moment. I made up my mind that I would hold on to nothing, that I would expect nothing, that henceforth I would live as an animal, a beast of prey, a rover, a plunderer.*"

WHAT COULD BE MORE EXISTENTIAL THAN INDISCRIMINATE SEX, PANHANDLING PARIS, AND PAPER TO WRITE ON?

The Beat Generation have often been referred to as America's version of existentialism, and indeed, Jack Kerouac's quotes of his main character Dean Moriarty (based on his real-life friend Neil Cassady) embeds the language of Heidegger in the jargon of the hipster. "Everything is fine, God exists, we know time. Everything since the Greeks has been predicated wrong. You can't make it with geometry and geometrical systems of thinking. It's all *this*..." says Moriarty. Driving feverishly, Moriarty launches into an existential soliloquy.

"*Oh, man! man! man!*" moaned Dean. "And it's not even the beginning of it—and now here we are at last going east together, we've never gone east together Sal, think of it, we'll dig Denver together and see what everybody's doing although that matters little to us, the point being that we know what IT is and we know TIME and we know that everything is really FINE." Then he whispered, clutching my sleeve, sweating, "Now you just dig them in front. They have worries, they're counting the miles, they're thinking about where to sleep tonight, how much money for gas, the weather, how they'll get there—and all the time they'll get there anyway, you see. but they need to worry and betray time with urgencies false and otherwise, purely anxious and whiny, their souls really won't be at peace unless they can latch on to an established and proven worry and having once found it they assume facial expressions to fit and go with it, which is, you see, unhappiness, and all the time it all flies by them and they know it and that too worries them no end."

AN AMERICAN, A CAR, AND AN OPEN ROAD WHAT COULD BE MORE EXISTENTIAL?

Beat literature flew in the face of traditional, straight-laced America, still under the sway of the Puritan heritage on the surface of the culture, masking the darker, wilder elements that always existed underneath.

Allen Ginsberg smacked Puritan and business-minded America on the skull with his epoch-making poem "Howl," and forced Americans to confront existential reality.

I saw the best minds of my generation destroyed by madness, starving hysterical naked,

dragging themselves through the negro streets at dawn looking for an angry fix,

angelheaded hipsters burning for the ancient heavenly connection to the starry dynamo in the machinery of night, who poverty and tatters and hollow-eyed and high sat up smoking in the supernatural darkness of cold-water flats floating across the tops of cities contemplating jazz,

who bared their brains to Heaven under the El and saw Mohammdean angels staggering on tenement roofs illuminated...

According to George Cotkin, author of *Existential America*, "Nearly everyone, it seemed, coming of age in 1950s and 1960s America danced to the song of French existentialism. 'I'd put on long black gloves ... smoke Camel cigarettes and read Sartre,' remembered Anne Rice, best-selling author of vampire tales. 'It felt terrific.' As a senior at the University of Michigan in 1956, poet and novelist Marge Piercy embraced existentialism to distance herself from bourgeois culture. Remembering photographs she had seen of Juliette Gréco – dark changeuse, friend of Sartre and Beauvoir, girlfriend of Miles Davis – Piercy adopted Gréco's style of dress: 'black jeans, a black turtleneck, my hair down and a lot of dark lipstick and eye make-up.' Existentialism extended into Piercy's politics, as she followed the leftist commitments of Sartre and Beauvoir. She was not alone. Civil rights activist Robert Moses, while jailed in Mississippi, reread Camus's *The Rebel* and *The Plague*. Moses stated, 'The main essence of what he says is what I feel real close to – closest to.' The meaning, excitement, and fashion of existentialism transformed the lives of many people."

Existential Politics

To define existential politics we return again to two existential principles: the importance of the individual in opposition to the tyranny of the collective, and the idea that action creates reality.

Through the '60s, as assassinations followed one after another, deaths in Vietnam rose, civil strife broke out on the streets of America, politics in America became existential.

As Norman Mailer put it at the time:

"*An existential political act, the drive by the Southern Negroes led by Martin Luther King to end segregation in restaurants in Birmingham, an act which is existential precisely because its end is unknown, has succeeded en route in discovering more of the American reality to us.*

If a public speaker in a midwestern town were to say, "J. Edgar Hoover has done more harm to the freedoms of America than Joseph Stalin," the act would be existential. Depending on the occasion and the town, he would be manhandled physically or secretly applauded, but he would create a new reality which would displace the old psychological reality that such a remark could not be made, even as for example the old Southern psychological reality that you couldn't get two Negroes to do anything together, let alone 2,000 has now been destroyed by a new and more accurate psychological reality: you can get 2,000 negroes to work in cooperation. The new psychological realities are closer to history and so closer to sanity and they exist because, and only because, the event has taken place..."

By the late 1960s, young Americans seemed far from the innocence of the 1950s. As young Americans faced the military draft that could pull them from their lives and send them to a deadly war in Asia for reasons that were never clearly explained, they collided head-on with the themes that preoccupied the existential writers. The possibility of an absurd death intruded upon their previously comfortable existence and the confrontation gave rise to a revolutionary movement in the generation. As Abbie Hoffman wrote in his book *Revolution for the Hell of It,* "Revolution for the hell of it? Why not? It's all a bunch of phony words anyway. Once one has experienced LSD, existential revolution, fought the intellectual game-playing of the individual in society, of one's identity, one realizes that action is the only reality; not only reality but morality as well. One learns reality is a subjective experience. It exists in my head. I am the Revolution."

Into the Sunset

The existentialism that exploded on the world in 1945 had been germinating for a century. The main reason it has always been so hard to define is that it was really a diverse reaction to challenges that were emerging in the progression of history. The exact nature of existentialism was not pre-determined, but the collisions of the forces that gave rise to it were inevitable. Man's view of the universe was expanding and old belief systems had to be revised to accommodate the changes. But essential to the realizations of existentialism was that no system is final in explaining and accommodating all that anyone actually experiences.

Existentialism was viewed by the philosophical establishment as a bastard movement, unworthy of being called philosophy, not a legitimate heir to the philosophical tradition. The philosophical establishment tended to look at the existentialists as a vulgar bunch of novelists and playwrights with philosophical pretensions. Typical of the establishment view was that of logical positivist Paul Edwards, a disciple and associate of Bertrand Russell, author of *The Logic of Moral Discourse*, editor of the eighth volume *Encyclopedia of Philosophy,* and the recipient of the Nicholas Murray Butler Silver Medal for distinguished contributions to philosophy. In a critique of Heidegger, Edwards scorned "the obscure and barbarous jargon of his writings and those of his followers" and said, "As philosophers these writers may be a failure, but as providers of mirth they are a huge success."

But in spite of traditional philosophy, existentialism established a place for itself in the history of philosophy and became arguably, as Paul Tillich said, "the style of our period in all realms of life" in the mid-twentieth century. The world has moved on, but the existentialists left their mark on all that was to follow them. Their influence spread far into the culture and into increasingly diverse realms and finally diffused. Existentialism had a profound influence cultural matrix of the twenty-first century world, and whatever comes in the future will have to deal with it.

Selected Bibliography

Barrett, William. *Irrational Man: A Study in Existential Philosophy.* Garden City, N.Y.: Doubleday Anchor Books, 1958.

Blackham, H.J. *Reality, Man and Existence: Essential Works of Existentialism.* New York: Bantam Books, 1965.

Camus, Albert. *Exile and the Kingdom.* New York: Alfred A. Knopf, 1957.

    The Myth of Sisyphus and Other Essays. New York: Vintage Books, 1955.

    Notebooks 1935-1942. New York. Harcourt, Brace, Jovanovich, 1963.

    Notebooks 1942-1951. New York. Harcourt, Brace, Jovanovich, 1965.

    The Rebel: An Essay on Man in Revolt. New York: Vintage Books, 1956

    Resistance, Rebellion and Death. New York: Alfred A. Knopf, 1960

    The Stranger. New York: Vintage Books, 1946.

Cotkin, George. *Existential America.* Baltimore and London: Johns Hopkins University Press, 2003.

Dostoyevsky, Fyodor. *Notes from Underground.* New York: Signet Classics, 1961.

    Crime and Punishment. New York: Bantam Books, 1958.

    The Brothers Karamazov. New York: Bantam Books, 1984.

    The Idiot. Baltimore, Md.: Penguin Books, 1955.

Friedman, Maurice, ed. *The Worlds of Existentialism: A Critical Reader.* New York: Random House, 1964.

Frankl, Victor E. *Man's Search for Meaning.* New York: Pocket Books, 1963.

Grene, Marjorie. *Introduction to Existentialism.* Chicago: University of Chicago Press, 1948.

Heidegger, Martin. *Being and Time.* Albany: State University of New York Press, 1996.

    Introduction to Metaphysics. New Haven: Yale University Press, 1959.

Discourse on Thinking. New York: Harper Perennial, 1969.

Heunemann, F.H. *Existentialism and the Modern Predicament.* New York: Harper and Brothers, 1958.

Hoffman, Abbie. *Revolution for the Hell of It.* New York: Dial Press, 1968.

Jaspers, Karl. *Reason and Existenz: Five Lectures.* Milwaukee: Marquette University Press, 1997.

Kafka, Franz. *The Metamorphosis.* New York: Bantam Books, 1972.

   The Trial. New York: Schocken Books, 1968.

Kauffmann, Walter, ed. *The Portable Nietzsche,* New York: Viking Press, 1954.

   Existentialism Dostoyevsky to Sartre. New York: Meridian Books, 1956.

Kaufmann, Walter, *From Shakespeare to Existentialism.* Garden City, N.Y. Doubleday Books, 1960.

Kierkegaard, Soren. *The Concept of Dread.* Princeton, N.J.: Princeton University Press, 1957.

   Concluding Unscientific Postscript. Princeton, N.J.: Princeton University Press, 1968.

   Either/Or. Princeton, N.J.: Princeton University Press, 1998.

   Fear and Trembling and *The Sickness Unto Death.* Garden City, N.Y. Doubleday Anchor Books, 1954.

Kerouac, Jack. *On the Road.* New York: Viking Press, 1955.

Laing, R.D. *The Politics of Experience.* New York: Ballantine Books, 1967.

Macquarrie, John. *Existentialism.* New York: Penguin Books, 1972.

Marcel, Gabriel. *The Philosophy of Existentialism.* New York: The Citadel Press, 1956.

Mailer, Norman. *The Presidential Papers of Norman Mailer.* New York: Bantam Books, 1964.

Miller, Henry. *Tropic of Cancer.* New York: Grove Press, 1961.

Molina, Fernando R., ed. *The Sources of Existentialism as Philosophy.* Englewood Cliffs, N.J.: Prentice Hall, 1956.

Nietzsche, Friedrich. *Joyful Wisdom* (alternately translated as: The Gay Science)

The Will to Power. New York: Vintage Books, 1967.

Thus Spake Zarathustra. New York: Penguin Books, 1977.

Reinhardt, Kurt F. *The Existential Revolt.* New York: Frederick Ungar Publishing, 1952.

Rilke, Rainer Maria. *The Notebooks of Malte Laurids Brigge.* New York: Vintage Books, 1990.

Sartre, Jean Paul. *Being and Nothingness.*

Existentialism and Human Emotions.

Existential Psychoanalysis. New York: Philosophical Library, 1953.

Nausea. New York: New Directions Publishing, 1964.

No Exit and Three Other Plays. New York: Vintage Books, 1989.

Troubled Sleep. New York: Vintage Books, 1951.

The War Diaries November 1939-March 1940. New York: Pantheon Books, 1985.

What is Literature? New York: Harper & Row, 1965.

Schopenhauer, Arthur. *Essays and Aphorisms.* New York. Penguin Books, 1970.

Solomon, Robert, ed. *Existentialism.* New York: Random House, 1974.

About the Author and Illustrator:

David Cogswell is a writer based in Hoboken, N.J. He has written thousands of articles on business, travel, politics, and the arts for various print and online publications, including *Online Journal, Democratic Underground, Bushwatch, Indymedia.org, Fortune.com, Travel Weekly,* the *Hudson Current* and the *Jersey Journal.* He's the author of *Chomsky For Beginners,* and has contributed pieces to a number of political books, including *Fortunate Son: The Making of an American President,* by J.H. Hatfield; *Ambushed: The Hidden History of the Bush Family* by Toby Rogers; and *America's Autopsy Report,* by John Kaminski. He is currently working on a book about corporatism.

Joe Lee is an illustrator, cartoonist, writer and clown. A graduate of Ringling Brothers, Barnum and Bailey's Clown College, he worked for many years as a circus clown. He is also the illustrator for many other For Beginners books including: *Dada and Surrealism For Beginners, Postmodernism For Beginners, Deconstruction For Beginners,* and *The Olympics For Beginners.* Joe lives with his wife, Mary Bess, three cats, and two dogs (Toby and Jack).

NOTES

NOTES

NOTES

NOTES

NOTES

NOTES

NOTES

NOTES

THE FOR BEGINNERS® SERIES

AFRICAN HISTORY FOR BEGINNERS:	ISBN 978-1-934389-18-8
ANARCHISM FOR BEGINNERS:	ISBN 978-1-934389-32-4
ARABS & ISRAEL FOR BEGINNERS:	ISBN 978-1-934389-16-4
ASTRONOMY FOR BEGINNERS:	ISBN 978-1-934389-25-6
BARACK OBAMA FOR BEGINNERS, AN ESSENTIAL GUIDE:	ISBN 978-1-934389-38-6
BLACK HISTORY FOR BEGINNERS:	ISBN 978-1-934389-19-5
THE BLACK HOLOCAUST FOR BEGINNERS:	ISBN 978-1-934389-03-4
BLACK WOMEN FOR BEGINNERS:	ISBN 978-1-934389-20-1
CHOMSKY FOR BEGINNERS:	ISBN 978-1-934389-17-1
DADA & SURREALISM FOR BEGINNERS:	ISBN 978-1-934389-00-3
DECONSTRUCTION FOR BEGINNERS:	ISBN 978-1-934389-26-3
DERRIDA FOR BEGINNERS:	ISBN 978-1-934389-11-9
EASTERN PHILOSOPHY FOR BEGINNERS:	ISBN 978-1-934389-07-2
EXISTENTIALISM FOR BEGINNERS:	ISBN 978-1-934389-21-8
FOUCAULT FOR BEGINNERS:	ISBN 978-1-934389-12-6
HEIDEGGER FOR BEGINNERS:	ISBN 978-1-934389-13-3
ISLAM FOR BEGINNERS:	ISBN 978-1-934389-01-0
KIERKEGAARD FOR BEGINNERS:	ISBN 978-1-934389-14-0
LINGUISTICS FOR BEGINNERS:	ISBN 978-1-934389-28-7
MALCOLM X FOR BEGINNERS:	ISBN 978-1-934389-04-1
NIETZSCHE FOR BEGINNERS:	ISBN 978-1-934389-05-8
THE OLYMPICS FOR BEGINNERS:	ISBN 978-1-934389-33-1
PHILOSOPHY FOR BEGINNERS:	ISBN 978-1-934389-02-7
PLATO FOR BEGINNERS:	ISBN 978-1-934389-08-9
POSTMODERNISM FOR BEGINNERS:	ISBN 978-1-934389-09-6
SARTRE FOR BEGINNERS:	ISBN 978-1-934389-15-7
SHAKESPEARE FOR BEGINNERS:	ISBN 978-1-934389-29-4
STRUCTURALISM & POSTRUCTURALISM FOR BEGINNERS:	ISBN 978-1-934389-10-2
ZEN FOR BEGINNERS:	ISBN 978-1-934389-06-5

www.forbeginnersbooks.com